How the Science of Psychology Gets Done

How the Science of Psychology Gets Done

Third Edition

Bruce B. Svare, Ph.D.

THOMSON

™

CUSTOM PUBLISHING

Editor: Julie Arkush
Publishing Services Supervisor: Christina Smith
Manufacturing Supervisor: Garris Blankenship
Project Coordinator: K.A. Espy
Graphic Designer: Krista Pierson
Rights and Permissions Specialist: Kalina Ingham Hintz
Marketing Manager: Sara L. Hinckley

Printed in the United States of America.

Thomson Custom Publishing
5191 Natorp Blvd.
Mason, Ohio 45040
USA

For information about our products, contact us:
1-800-355-9983
http://www.thomsoncustom.com

International Headquarters
Thomson Learning
International Division
290 Harbor Drive, 2nd Floor
Stamford, CT 06902-7477
USA

UK/Europe/Middle East/South Africa
Thomson Learning
Berkshire House
168-173 High Holborn
London WCIV 7AA

Asia
Thomson Learning
60 Albert Street, #15-01
Albert Complex
Singapore 189969

Canada
Nelson Thomson Learning
1120 Birchmount Road
Toronto, Ontario MIK 5G4
Canada
United Kingdom

Visit us at www.thomsoncustom.com and learn more about this book and other titles published by Thomson Learning Custom Publishing.

ISBN 0-759-31880-8

The Adaptable Courseware Program consists of products and additions to existing Custom Publishing products that are produced from camera-ready copy. Peer review, class testing, and accuracy are primarily the responsibility of the author(s).

I dedicate this book to my father
Myron Louis Svare

Contents

Preface   ix

Part I   FOUNDATIONS

1 *An Overview*   3

2 *The Evolution of a Scientist*   5

3 *An Observation That Provoked 25 Years of Research*   11

4 *Getting Grants to Do Research*   17

Part II   PRELIMINARY WORK

5 *Description of Aggressive Behavior and Basic Physiology*   25

6 *Examining the Importance of the Young for Postpartum Aggressive Behavior*   29

7 *Determining Where to Go Next*   35

Part III   SEEKING PHYSIOLOGICAL UNDERPINNINGS

8 *The Search for a Hormonal Substrate During Pregnancy*   41

9 *Additional Questions and Shades of Gray Regarding Pregnancy-Induced Aggression*   47

10 *Searching for a Biological Substrate for Postpartum Docility*   49

11 *Searching for the Biological Underpinnings of
        Postpartum Aggression*   55

Part IV UNDERSTANDING
INDIVIDUAL VARIATION

12 *Why Study Individual Differences?*   73

13 *The Important Role of Genes in Shaping Individual
        Variation in Agression*   77

14 *Prior Intrauterine Position Can Also Explain Individual
        Variation in Female Aggressive Behavior*   85

15 *Influence of the Prenatal Hormone Environment on the
        Development of Female Aggressive Behaviors*   91

PART V PROXIMATE AND ULTIMATE CAUSATION

16 *How Do Physiological Changes Mediate Alterations
        in Female Aggressive Behavior?*   103

17 *Summarizing What We Know About the Proximate
        Causes of Female Aggressive Behavior*   109

18 *Considering Questions of Ultimate Causation: Female
        Aggression Viewed as an Optimization Problem*   113

19 *Putting It All Together: Why is the Study of Female
        Aggressive Behavior Important?*   119

20 *Some Final Thoughts*   123

        Chronological List of Publications   125

        Index   129

Preface

THE FIELD OF psychology prides itself on being a discipline that encourages empirical inquiry by using the most rigorous scientific methodology available to its professionals. In this sense, psychology is no different than biology, physics, mathematics or chemistry. However, it can be argued that the nature of what psychologists study, behavioral responses, is far more complex than the subject matter of a chemist, biologist, mathematician, or physicist. While this complexity makes psychological inquiry enormously challenging, it is also responsible for fueling the discipline in new and exciting directions. Indeed, there is no other field of scientific inquiry where there is so much uncharted territory still awaiting exploration. The study of behavior is truly still in its infancy.

How the Science of Psychology Gets Done: One Researcher's Journey was motivated by my desire to engage new students of psychology in the actual discovery process so that they could more fully appreciate how an actual research psychologist receives his training and then goes about his work. Students that are new to the study of behavior often do not understand just how a research hypothesis is formulated. Moreover, they do not fully appreciate the day to day rigor of behavioral research, the ups and downs from success and failure, the constant pressure to obtain funding and resource support, and generally what goes on behind the scenes to advance psychological research. By drawing upon my own experiences in the laboratory, it is my hope that you will more fully appreciate the process of science in the fascinating and often unpredictable field of behavioral inquiry that we call psychology.

There are many to thank for their inspiration and help along the way. My undergraduate mentors at Susquehanna University, Jim Misanin and Z. Michael Nagy, initially inspired me to become

a research psychologist and seek graduate training. Doug Cand-
land and Alan Leshner at Bucknell University, lead me to a greater
understanding of experimental psychology and animal behavior
during my preparation for a Master's degree. At Rutgers University during my doctoral training, Ron Gandelman taught me more
about behavioral endocrinology and reproductive physiology.
During postdoctoral training at the Worcester Foundation for Experimental Biology, Andrzej Bartke and Foetus Macrides taught
me the latest techniques in endocrine assay methods and the quan-
tification of hormones in blood and tissue. To all of them I owe a
great debt of gratitude for their wisdom and patience during my
training as a research psychologist.

Graduate students provide the backbone for psychological research and I have been very fortunate to have the very best our discipline has to offer. Martha Mann, Craig Kinsley, John Broida, Joe
Miele, Loraina Ghiraldi, and Mike Boechler have all contributed
with sweat and inspired thinking throughout their training. Also,
undergraduate students Chris Konen-Wagner, Owen Samuels, Bar-
bara Nield, Marshall Garland, Debbie Katz, and Greg Jason have
played important roles in data collection and analysis. Much of the
research discussed here could not have been done without the
dedicated "team" efforts of those listed above.

I also thank my colleagues in the biopsychology program at
SUNY-Albany. Robert Rosellini, Gordon Gallup, Bruce Dudek,
Bruce McCutcheon, and Cheryl Frye have been unselfish with their
time and supportive of my ideas.

The research reported here was supported in part by the National Institute of Mental Health (NIMH), the National Institute
of Aging (NIA), the National Institute of Drug Abuse (NIDA), the
National Science Foundation (NSF), and the Harry Frank
Guggenheim Foundation. I am indebted to those granting agencies for supporting the science conducted in my laboratory.

Finally, to my wonderful wife Maryalice, and to my two fine sons
Mark and John, thanks for letting me indulge myself in something
that I love to do!

Bruce Svare
SUNY-Albany

How the Science of Psychology Gets Done

Part I

FOUNDATIONS

1

An Overview

HAVING TAUGHT introductory psychology now for over 25 years, I have often felt that new students to the discipline have a hard time understanding the process that most typical scientists go through in researching a problem. This is particularly regrettable in the case of psychology, where new scientific methods have promoted exciting and unparalleled advances in the study of behavior. Rigorous laboratory-based research is the true lifeblood of the discipline today. One must understand the process of how it is done in order to appreciate the resulting outcome of the pursuit.

Psychology is dynamic and more grounded in empirical, laboratory-based scientific methods than ever before. At one time, our discipline was considered "soft" and not rigorous in comparison to biology, chemistry, and physics—the so-called "hard" sciences. This label has dramatically changed over the past 30 years to the point where the tactics used by psychologists are now considered to be every bit as rigorous as those used by scientists in other disciplines. To fully appreciate psychology as the modern discipline that it is today, it is incumbent upon new students to understand the techniques and methods of laboratory-based research.

In a typical psychology 101 class, students are required to read a textbook and listen to lectures on the study of behavior. The information they are given represents only the end product or final results of many years of painstaking and often monotonous research conducted by thousands of psychologists working in laboratories around the world. Not represented are the disappointments, the wrong choices, the meaningless results, the accidental discoveries, and the slow, incremental process that provides answers but simultaneously provokes many more questions along the way.

When science is practiced at its most basic level, failures often far exceed successes and the route to true discovery and meaningful information on a research topic is long and arduous. New students rarely see this part of psychology. As a result, their perception of the discipline and the scientific process is limited and often terribly biased to a few unfortunate stereotypes.

With this in mind, the relative misunderstanding that new students of psychology have regarding the process of science in psychology, I have taken it upon myself to write this book. The simple goal that I had in mind was to help new students to the discipline more fully appreciate how an actual psychologist is trained and then goes about researching a problem.

I can think of no better way to accomplish this goal than to tell you about the research I have been conducting for the last 25 years. I will do so in the most non-technical way I know by limiting the use of jargon and scientific language. Hopefully, you will find this to be both informative and interesting and you will have a better view of how a psychologist working in a research setting actually goes about his business.

2

The Evolution of a Scientist

AFTER A RATHER undistinguished high school career in Gardner, Massachusetts where I spent most of my time playing sports and very little of my time studying, I attended Susquehanna University in beautiful central Pennsylvania. I bounced around from major to major, going from math to biology to sociology. Nothing really interested me all that much although I managed to do pretty well in the courses I took. I took Introductory Psychology my sophomore year, absolutely hated the professor and the material, and barely eked out a grade of C–!

In my sophomore year of college, I lived in a fraternity where there were a number of older students who majored in psychology. Not only did they live and breathe the subject, but also they were very involved in the experimental side of the discipline. Several of them worked with professors who were studying animal learning and memory. They were actively involved in the psychology department's animal laboratory where they took care of the animals, ran the research, analyzed the data, and assisted in writing up the results for publications.

A number of the older students went so far as to give talks on their research at national meetings and publish their findings in psychology journals. I got to know these students very well but more importantly I began to go to the laboratory with them and watch what they were doing.

I also became friendly with the two experimental psychologists on the faculty, Dr. James Misanin and Dr. Michael Nagy. These two scientists more than anyone stimulated my interest in psychology and the experimental side of the discipline. Soon I was assisting in the laboratory, and my passion for experimental psychology grew as I gained more exposure to the discipline.

My appetite for conducting basic research in psychology seemed to grow each day as I learned more and more about how to design, conduct and analyze psychological experiments. Indeed, I even started thinking that perhaps I had found my future and that I would become a psychologist some day.

During the summers of my junior and senior years at Susquehanna, I worked full time as a research assistant on grants that were funded by the National Science Foundation and the National Institute of Mental Health. It was a great experience working with these professors on their research projects and learning more about how to do science. It also solidified my desire to go to graduate school and receive advanced training in psychology.

I graduated with a Bachelor of Arts degree from Susquehanna in 1971 and immediately entered a masters program in experimental psychology at Bucknell University. I was fortunate to receive a National Institute of Mental Health Traineeship, which provided me with a small stipend to live on and, more importantly, paid for my tuition at Bucknell.

I was privileged at the time to work with a psychologist, Dr. Alan Leshner, who specialized in studying how hormones influence social behavior (called a "behavioral endocrinologist"). Dr Leshner has gone on to great distinction in that he is now the Director of the National Institute of Drug Abuse (NIDA). While in his laboratory, I became keenly interested in studying the biology of aggressive behavior. My master's thesis under his direction was designed to examine the relationship between hormones, fear, and aggression in laboratory mice.

After receiving my Masters degree in psychology at Bucknell in 1973, I continued my education in psychology at Rutgers University where I received a research assistantship for three years and studied in their doctoral program in biopsychology. Simply put, biopsychology is the study of how our biology influences our behavior. I received my doctoral training under the direction of Dr. Ronald Gandelman, a behavioral endocrinologist who was also very interested in the effects of hormones on social and reproductive behavior.

My doctoral dissertation involved an assessment of how hormones influence various aspects of maternal behavior in female mice shortly after they deliver their offspring and are caring for them. In 1976 I completed my course work, successfully defended my dissertation, and received my Doctor of Philosophy degree from Rutgers.

Psychologists trained in the field of biopsychology often must learn a number of advanced techniques in biology and chemistry in order to answer research questions. To continue in the field of research that I was pursuing, I felt that it was necessary to receive additional training in an institution where the latest and most advanced techniques were being used on a regular basis. I applied for and received a National Institute of Health Postdoctoral Fellowship to study at the Worcester Foundation for Experimental Biology in Massachusetts.

While at the Worcester Foundation, I worked with a world renown endocrinologist by the name of Dr. Andrzej Bartke. He

Figure 1. The subjects used in biopsychology experiments.

taught me how to quantify the level of various hormones in the blood and brain tissue of laboratory animals. I was fortunate to spend 2 and ½ years under his direction since I was able to devote all my time and energy to conducting research and learning new endocrinological techniques. Ultimately these techniques proved to be very important for much of the research I would conduct in my future career.

Postdoctoral research appointments do not last forever and it was time for me to move on. I came to SUNY-Albany as an Assistant Professor of Psychology in 1978, was promoted to Associate Professor with tenure in 1982, and was promoted to Full Professor in 1987. SUNY-Albany has been an ideal place for me to combine my research and teaching interests. I have continued an active research program focusing on how hormones influence our social and reproductive behaviors.

Figure 2. The laboratory team that conducted much of the research in Dr. Svare's laboratory at SUNY-Albany. From left to right Dr. Martha Mann, Dr. John Broida, Dr. Joseph Miele, Dr. Loraina Ghiraldi, Dr. Craig Kinsley. Absent, Dr. Michael Boechler.

I have been lucky to have had a number of very good graduate students who have received their doctoral training under my direction and have now gone on to their own research and academic careers. Their contributions to the research story presented here have played a pivotal role in many of our discoveries.

To name a few of those students who are now established professionals: Dr. Martha Mann is an associate professor of psychology at the University of Texas at Arlington, Dr. John Broida is an associate professor of psychology at the University of Southern Maine in Portland, Dr. Craig Kinsley is an associate professor of psychology at the University of Richmond, Dr. Loraina Ghiraldi is an associate professor of psychology at St. Lawrence University, Dr. Joseph Miele is an assistant professor of psychology at East Stroudsburg State University, and Dr. Michael Boechler is a postdoctoral research associate in the biology department at the University of Missouri at Columbia.

In addition, I have also taken on numerous undergraduate students through the years and have trained them in laboratory-based research in psychology. A number of them have gone on into medical school and have become doctors while others have gone on into the sciences, including psychology, and are now faculty members at other institutions.

I have enjoyed the challenge of teaching SUNY-Albany undergraduate and graduate students who, for the most part, are intelligent and energetic in their pursuit of a good education. Typically, I teach introductory psychology, honors tutorial in psychology, as well as a graduate course in my specialty, behavioral endocrinology.

3

An Observation That Provoked 25 Years of Research

"To what degree should my choice of research work be governed by human needs, by social imperatives, and how am I to justify spending all of my energies on any research that does not bear directly on pressing human problems. The solution, or rationalization, that I have finally come up with is that it is a perfectly worthwhile way of spending one's own life to do your level best to increase human knowledge, and it is not necessary nor is it always even desirable to be constrained by possible applicability of what you find to immediate problems. This may sound peculiar to some people, but it is a value judgement which I myself have made and which I can live with."

Frank Beach (From G. Lindzey, 1974 *A History of Psychology in Autobiography*, Vol. 5, Prentice-Hall, Englwood-Cliffs, New Jersey).

THE QUOTATION ABOVE from one of psychology's pioneering scientists captures my own underlying motivation for doing research in the field I have chosen. The science I have conducted has never been influenced by anything except my own fascination with understanding how something works. I came upon a phenomena that was intrinsically interesting and I wanted to learn more about it; I did not even give one moment of thought to what its possible social or practical implications might be. This being said, let me take you through the chronology of events that unfolded when I first discovered a phenomena that eventually came to dominate my career in science.

For many years, I have been consumed with the study of aggressive behavior in mammals. In particular, I have focused much of my attention on the ability of female mammals to exhibit intense aggression during certain periods of their reproductive cycle, especially shortly after they have given birth to their young.

Why I selected female aggressive behavior as a research topic is important for your understanding of how science frequently gets done in psychology. It was purely a chance observation that led me to spend so many years researching this topic. Importantly, my fascination with female aggressive behavior had little practical relevance at the time to solving any major human problem.

I was curious with how the behavior worked, what controlled it, why it appeared at some times and not at others, what physiological and environmental factors were important for its display and so on. I was not in the least bit interested in questions of application. I was satisfied only in determining just how and why the behavior occurred in such a dramatic fashion.

Throughout my research career, I have maintained what is called a continuous breeding colony of outbred Rockland-Swiss (R-S) albino mice. That is to say, I would breed all of my own mice for my research. This was done for many different reasons. The most important factor however was related to my involvement with developmental research. In this kind of research, it is critical to control the conditions of the experiment from the time the animals are conceived to the time they are used as experimental subjects. Purchasing animals from a supplier therefore is not a viable alternative.

As was typical in our laboratory and other laboratories that are classified as continuous breeding colonies, female mice were placed into a cage of their own (they were isolated) after they had been impregnated by a male mouse.

Pregnancy in the mouse is easily detected by what is called a vaginal plug. After a male mouse has intercourse with a female mouse, he leaves semen in her vagina and it hardens over night. If the vagina of the female is examined, the plug is clearly seen and it is almost 100% certain that she is pregnant. The pregnancy period (called gestation) is 18 days long in the mouse.

When the mother delivers on the evening of the 18th day of gestation, she usually gives birth to anywhere from 4 to over 20 offspring in some cases. A mother mouse nurses her offspring and produces milk for them through a process called lactation. Postpartum female mice nurse their young and exhibit lactation for about 15 days. By the 21st to 25th day, her young are ready to fend for themselves and go off on their own. This is called "weaning" and in most continuous breeding mouse laboratories, offspring are separated from their mother around the 21st day of life.

By accident one day, I placed a male mouse into the cage of a female that had delivered her young 5 days earlier. What I saw I could not believe as the nursing mother mouse leaped off of her offspring and viciously attacked the male mouse! She would not give up and ferociously bit the male every chance she had.

The male mouse ran around the cage trying to get away from the attacking mother, never defended himself or fought back, and apparently could do nothing to stem the tide of biting attacks delivered by the mother. Eventually the male mouse, all bloodied and beaten to a pulp, would just cower in the corner of the cage in a submissive posture and would just "take it".

The ferocity of the attacking behavior by the female absolutely amazed me since I had tested females for their reactions to males in many other experiments and had always found that they were quite social and never would attack a male or another female for that matter.

The one important difference of course was the fact that all of my previous work involved female mice that had not been in the reproductive state of lactation. That is to say, they had not gone through 19 days of pregnancy and experienced child birth and the nursing of young. All the females I had examined for aggressive responses in other work were females that were classified as virgins. They had not mated with males and otherwise were in a non-reproductive state.

Most scientists believed at this time that there were huge sex differences in the display of aggressive behavior. Indeed, almost all of the research conducted to this point supported the notion that males were pretty much predisposed to be aggressive and nasty while females were wired to be docile and nurturing.

Figures 3-4. A typical example of postpartum aggression in the mouse. A lactating female mouse, having delivered her offspring four days earlier, encountering a strange male mouse that has entered her nest site. The female briefly sniffs the male (top figure) and then within seconds launches a vicious biting attack toward the male (bottom figure). Note that the male has been striped with a black magic marker.

Laboratory research on many types of mammals showed that males were very aggressive against one another while females were very social and never attacked other males or females. Importantly, none of this research ever tested females during other reproductive states such as when they were pregnant or when they were nursing their young!

I pored over the literature on aggressive behavior and could find nothing on female aggression except a few vague references to "maternal defense." Indeed, many of the authors of these reports spoke as if the topic had been well-researched in many different mammalian species. In fact, the only information that I could find was a few anecdotal (nonscientific) reports of zoo keepers and dog breeders. These references frequently would mention that it is a good idea to stay away from mothers nursing their young since they can get pretty nasty and bite your head off!

I realized that I had, by chance, stumbled upon a behavioral phenomena that no one had studied experimentally and, hence, no one really knew anything about. At this point, I would say that I didn't really care so much about what the immediate or long-term implications of studying this behavior might be. What I did know was that it looked pretty darn interesting. I was fascinated at how the female's behavior could change so rapidly from being docile during the virgin non-reproductive state to marked aggressiveness after giving birth.

What I also found interesting was the fact that so many before me had concluded that the female brain just wasn't wired for exhibiting a "masculine" behavior like aggression. Obviously, I thought, they just hadn't studied the female at the right time for if they had looked at females after they had given birth, they would have found that they are every bit as aggressive as males if not more so.

The study of female aggressive behavior therefore came to dominate my research interests. However, like most scientists, I have also maintained a steady interest in other areas. Partly due to my own interests and partly due to those of my students, I have also published research in the area of sexual differentiation, puberty, paternal behavior, learning and memory, feeding and drinking, and sexual behavior. Importantly, however, over 80% of my research time has been devoted to studying female aggressive behavior.

4

Getting Grants to Do Research

As NOTED EARLIER, a careful examination of the scientific literature in biology, psychology, zoology, and animal behavior revealed
little if any information regarding aggressive behavior exhibited by
female mammals. Intrigued by this gap in our knowledge, I
thought my next step should be the development of a federal grant
application for support of this research topic. The nuts and bolts
of that process can be quite mysterious and daunting to the unini-
tiated so let me briefly discuss how it is done in the United States.

I have submitted many grant applications in my years as a research psychologist. Indeed, I have been very fortunate to have received grants for research on female aggressive behavior from the
National Science Foundation (NSF), the National Institute of
Mental Health (NIMH), the National Institute of Health (NIH),
the National Institute of Drug Abuse (NIDA), the National Institute of Aging (NIA), and the Guggenheim Foundation. The need
for such grants and the process itself is an important one to understand since it is really the lifeblood of scientific progress in our
country.

A good beginning question might be: Why does one need grant
money in order to do research? The answer to that question is very
simple. Research, especially with animals, is very expensive. While
some types of research in psychology do not require large amounts

of money, biopsychological experimentation with animals usually requires some funding.

Every institution, SUNY-Albany included, charges its investigators money to feed and house research animals. This is called "cage charges" or "per diems". Additionally, technicians to care for the animals and run the experiments are needed and can be very costly. It is also necessary to hire postdoctoral, graduate, and undergraduate students to help run experiments. On top of this, supplies for biological and chemical work can be very expensive and this too must be paid for by grant money. Add on to this computing time for statistical analyses, purchase of computers, printers and other essential equipment, overhead and fringe benefits for staff and secretarial time, and grant applications can soar very easily into several hundred thousand dollars. Everything must be paid for—there are no free rides!

Most grant applications require many months of hard work and extensive revision and rewriting. The application form for most granting agencies includes sections requiring extensive historical and conceptual background information as well as detailed explanations and rationales for research methods, planned experiments and anticipated results. The grant application also must include subject and budget justifications and biographical information on all investigators and their respective roles in the proposed work. Approvals and letters of support must also be obtained from outside collaborators as well as university personnel such as department chairs, college deans, and sponsored funds administrators.

Executing a good grant application is almost always a very time consuming task and ordinarily requires many months of hard work and extensive revision and rewriting. Indeed, most scientists I know would rather be in the laboratory doing research as opposed to spending the inordinate amount of time that it takes to write and submit an application that will be successful.

Grant applications are reviewed four times a year by specialists selected by the US government. These groups are called study sections and there are hundreds of them manned by our most distinguished scientists. Study section members are not paid to do their work but instead volunteer their time to serve the scientific community and the pursuit of knowledge in our country. They must decide the scientific merit of a proposal and they do so by evaluating the applicants training, previous productivity and, most importantly, the proposal's scientific soundness and originality.

Study sections can approve or disapprove a grant. Approved grants are assigned a priority score by the members of the study section. Only the best priority scores—those in the upper 5%—ever get funded. Oftentimes then, approved grants that have good, but not spectacular, priority scores are turned back to the applicants with encouragement to resubmit a revised application for another review cycle.

Like most scientists, I have had my share of heartaches and disappointments along the way. For example, before I received my first grant for work on female aggression, I had to resubmit the application 4 times because the reviewers on the study section did not like some of the experiments I had proposed. It ordinarily takes about 3 or 4 months to write an application and then another 6 months to have it reviewed. You can see then, that it can take a considerable period of time between the creation of an idea (a hypothesis) and ultimately receiving a grant to do the research.

Luckily, I finally received a grant to do the research I had proposed, but only after I had convinced my study section that my work was worthy and would result in meaningful information. Grants usually last 2 or 3 years and then it is time to apply again and go through the same process.

If your work is going well and you are publishing good data, the chances are you will stand a reasonable chance of being renewed for another 3 years. However, if you are going down too many blind alleys and the scientific review panel thinks that you're not making enough progress, the chances are you might have to resubmit another application and therefore have a break in your funding. This happens to almost all scientists at one time or another and it causes turmoil since you are left scrambling to find alternate sources of support for your laboratory while you are resubmitting your grant and waiting to hear about a renewal during the next cycle of reviews.

Sometimes the university will pay your expenses for the interim and sometimes it will not. In academia it is referred to as "bridge" money and it is word that no one really likes to hear since usually it has overtones of uncertainly and anxiety.

I have known many scientists who have had to pay for their research out of their own pocket for extended periods of time while waiting to hear about a grant. Often it is necessary to scale back your operation (e.g., let people go, reduce the size of your animal colony, do less research) until you can get funding again. All of this can cause great stress and anxiety since you are almost constantly in the process of applying for grants and/or waiting to hear about grants.

Current statistics show that only about 1 out of every 10 research grants is successful (that is, the granting agency ultimately funds the grant). As noted earlier, grants oftentimes are approved but not funded which essentially means that there is not enough money for the application to be funded in the present cycle. The author of such an application would usually be encouraged to resubmit the grant with significant changes suggested by the review panel.

It is not uncommon to hear of grant proposals being resubmitted 7, 8, or 9 times before they are actually approved and funded. The outcome of this process is that only the very best research proposals ultimately get funded in the United States. However, persistence, the willingness to revise an application extensively to make it more appealing to the review panel, and a little bit of luck is also important to success. While it is survival of the fittest at its most evolved level, there simply is no substitute for a great scientific idea that is combined with dogged determination and sweat.

One final note regarding research grants. There simply isn't enough money out there for the many dedicated scientists that compete each year for the limited amount of money available. As a result, there are many excellent grant proposals with truly creative ideas that never get a stitch of money. Is this something that will change in the near future with a dramatic injection of more money? That is a question which is difficult to answer. My guess is that as long as there is not peace and harmony in the world then things will continue on as they have. The combined research budget for NIH, NIMH, and NSF is less than 1% of the entire defense department budget or approximately 1 cruise missile.

As much as you may want to think that our country values research and education, a very good argument can be made that it values our military much more. The dollar figures simply do not lie in telling us where the priorities are in our country. While federal funds spent on research by the US government is certainly significant, it pales in comparison to what is expended each year on defending our country.

Part II
PRELIMINARY WORK

5

Description of Aggressive Behavior and Basic Physiology

ONCE I RECEIVED my first research grant, my goal was to characterize the aggressive behavior seen during pregnancy and lactation as best as possible. Descriptive analysis of behavior, regardless of whether laboratory animals or humans are the subjects of study, is always the preliminary step that a psychologist must conduct before moving on to more complicated questions of underlying causation.

Experiments that we conducted at this stage were quite simple (Svare and Gandelman, 1973; Mann, Konen & Svare, 1984; Mann & Svare, 1982; Svare, 1983; Mann and Svare, 1983; Svare, Betteridge, Katz, & Samuels, 1981; Ghiraldi, Plonsky, & Svare, 1993). For example, in one study we took a number of virgin female R-S mice that had reached adult life (about 60 days of age), mated and then isolated them in standard mouse cages after we found a vaginal plug, and tested them for their reaction to an adult male mouse every few days as they went through pregnancy and lactation.

With pregnancy lasting 18 days and lactation lasting 21 days, the experiment lasted a total of almost 40 days. Simultaneous with this, we also took other females that had been mated and we collected blood from them. We performed what is called radioimunoassay on the blood to allow us to detect hormone levels in the blood. This was done so that we could determine what hormonal changes were going on in the female as she went through pregnancy and lactation (See Figure 5 below).

You may ask, what is the purpose of looking at hormone levels in these animals? As you are probably aware, hormones have a great deal to due with reproduction in mammals including the human. Ovarian hormones (estrogen and progesterone) support the fetus in the uterus during pregnancy. The hormone prolactin, which is secreted from the pituitary gland, is essential for the

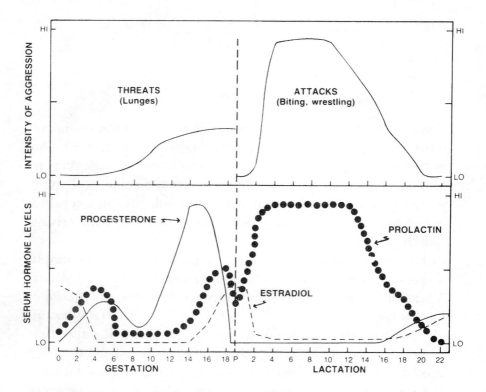

Figure 5. The relationship between hormones and maternal aggression in the mouse. The figure shows the intensity of aggressive behavior (top) and serum hormone levels (bottom) of Rockland-Swiss (R-S) albino mice throughout pregnancy and lactation. The physiological and behavioral data are a composite of information collected in the author's laboratory, as well as other laboratories.

process called lactation (the production and secretion of milk). Once the pregnant female delivers her young and begins to nurse, prolactin secretions stimulate the formation of milk in the mammary glands.

Hormones also are known to be implicated in many behavioral processes in both lower animals and in humans. The magnitude of this involvement varies from species to species. But the field of biopsychology and, more specifically behavioral endocrinology, has generated important information regarding the involvement of ovarian hormones in sexual and maternal behaviors as well as learning, feeding, and drinking. Thus, given their rapid changing status in females as they go through pregnancy and lactation, we wanted to explore possible relationships between hormonal changes and changes in aggressive behavior.

In these initial studies, we found that aggression is first observed in the form of threat behavior during mid-pregnancy (10th day of gestation (pregnancy)) with peak levels of threats seen toward the end pregnancy. We called aggressive behavior observed during gestation "pregnancy-induced aggression" to distinguish it from the more intense aggression that we observed after the mother gave birth to her young and was nursing them.

As can be seen in Figure 5, late pregnant females typically exhibited threat behaviors; these responses consist of rapid lunges toward the intruder male that fall short of actual physical contact. Although attacks consisting of biting and wrestling are also occasionally displayed by late pregnant females, the primary mode of aggressive responding seen during pregnancy is that of threat behaviors.

Immediately following delivery of young (an event called parturition), we found that aggression by females was virtually absent for several days. This is interesting because it corresponds to a reproductive period in mammals called postpartum estrous. This is a time when the female is reproductively ready to mate and become pregnant again. Indeed, this is the case in mammals living in the wild—they often will mate again right after they deliver a litter. It is not unusual to see mammals in the wild simultaneously pregnant and nursing a litter of pups at the same time.

After females nurse their young for a few days however, they become intensely aggressive and we referred to this as "postpartum or maternal aggression". The intense attacking behavior gradually peaks between days 4 and 10 of lactation. This form of aggressive behavior is very ferocious and consists of rapid biting attacks on the intruder. With advancing lactation and the growth of young, lactating females exhibit a dramatic reduction in the intensity of their behavior to a point where there is little postpartum aggression observed around the time when young are weaned (21st day of lactation).

When we examined the hormonal changes occurring in the mouse, we found a number of striking endocrine changes that seemed to correspond to changes in aggression. For example, when threat behavior was very low during early pregnancy, progesterone values were also very low. Also, when prolactin levels were at their highest level during lactation, postpartum aggression also was at its highest. Periods of low prolactin (early and late lactation) corresponded to periods when little aggression was observed. Could it be, we thought, that aggression during pregnancy was progesterone dependent while aggression during lactation was prolactin dependent? This is a question that we returned to later on in our research program.

6

Examining the Importance of the Young for Postpartum Aggressive Behavior

IN ADDITION TO performing descriptive analyses of possible hormone behavior correlations, we also performed some other simple experiments to look at the relationship between the presence or absence of the mother's offspring and her aggressive behavior during lactation (Svare, 1977; Svare and Gandelman, 1973).

In one study lactating female mice were divided into three groups on the 4th day following the delivery of young. The animals from one group were tested for aggression after their pups had been removed for 1 hour while the animals from a second group were tested for aggression 5 hours after their young had been removed. The remaining animals were tested for aggression immediately after their young were removed. The results showed that aggression was exhibited by almost every animal in the groups tested 0 or 1 hr after pup removal but was seldom observed in animals tested 5 hours after their pups were removed (See Table 1, following page).

Since aggressive behavior was eliminated following the removal of young, we reasoned that it could be restored by reintroducing pups to the mother. To examine this possibility, lactating mice had their young removed from the cage for 5 hours on Postpartum Day 4. Following the 5 hour period of pup removal, mothers from one

TABLE 1. THE INFLUENCE OF PUP REMOVAL ON
MATERNAL AGGRESSION

	Duration (Hr) of Pup Removal	
0	*1*	*5*
12/12(100)	11/12(91)	2/12(16)

The proportion (and percentage) of aggressive lactating mice that attacked a mouse intruder after their young were removed either for 0, 1, or 5 hr on Postpartum Day 4. Twelve animals comprised each group.
(From Svare and Gandelman, 1973)

group were tested for aggression against a male intruder after they had been reunited with their pups for 10 minutes. Mothers from a second group were tested for aggression 5 minutes after having been reunited with their young. The animals from a final group were not presented with young and were tested immediately after the 5-hour period of pup removal. The results of this experiment showed almost all of the mother mice tested for aggression 10 or 5 minutes following the reintroduction of young attacked the intruder male while animals not given young following the 5 hour period of separation never fought (See Table 2).

In the experiment outlined above, we observed that the reinstatement of maternal aggression in postpartum females was not related to the exhibition of maternal activities such as retrieval of the young, licking of the young, or assuming a nursing posture over the young. Indeed, we noticed that aggression frequently was

TABLE 2. THE INFLUENCE OF PUP REINSTATEMENT ON
MATERNAL AGGRESSION

	Duration (min) of Pup Replacement	
10	*5*	*0*
10/10(100)	7/10(70)	0/10(00)

The proportion and percentage of aggressive lactating mice that attacked an intruder following 0, 5, or 10 min of pup replacement. The lactating animals first had their pups removed for 5 hr prior to pup replacement. Ten animals comprised each group.
(From Svare and Gandelman, 1973)

observed in females that never came into direct contact with their young. Therefore, we reasoned that direct physical contact between the mother and her young may not be necessary for maternal aggressive behavior to be maintained once the female has been nursing her young for a few days.

We examined this possibility by testing the aggressiveness of postpartum female mice whose pups had been placed behind a wire mesh partition in the homecage of the female for a period of 5 hours on the fourth postpartum day. Therefore, these mothers could see, hear, and smell their young but they could not have direct physical contact with them. Control groups consisted of animals that either had their pups completely removed for 5 hours or were allowed to remain with them. Animals that were permitted direct physical contact with young or that had their pups placed on the opposite side of a partition for 5 hours were very aggressive while animals that had their pups completely removed never fought (see Table 3). This finding confirmed our expectation and clearly showed that aggression can be maintained, at least for short periods of time, in the absence of any direct physical contact between the mother and her young.

The functional significance of the findings reviewed above would seem to be very important. The fact that contact with young is not critical for the short-term maintenance of aggressive behavior in postpartum mice may have important implications for other aspects of parental behavior. For example, foraging behavior is of

TABLE 3. THE EXTEROCEPTIVE MAINTENANCE OF MATERNAL AGGRESSION

	Condition of Pups	
Pups in Direct Contact	*Pups Behind Partition*	*Pups Completely Removed*
10/10(100)	8/10(80)	0/10(00)

The proportion and percentage of aggressive lactating animals that attacked an adult intruder following 5 hr of direct contact, complete removal, or placement of their pups behind a wire partition in their cage. Ten animals comprised each group.
(From Svare and Gandelman, 1973)

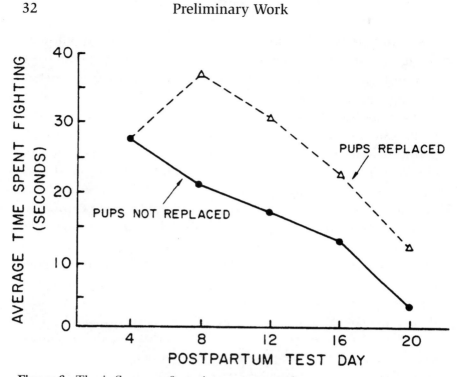

Figure 6. The influence of continuous pup replacement on postpartum aggression in the mouse. The figure shows the average time spent fighting (seconds) on Postpartum Days 4-20 for aggressive lactating R-S females that had their young repeatedly replaced with newborn young and for animals whose young were not replaced. All animals were pre-tested for aggression on Postpartum Day 4, following which separate groups of animals either had their young replaced with 1-day-old pups or left undisturbed. Posttests for aggression and pup replacement were conducted at four-day intervals on Postpartum Days 8, 12, 16 and 20. Each test was 3 minutes in duration (Svare, 1977).

obvious importance to both the mother and her young during this period. Time constraints on foraging behavior may be regulated by the young in the sense that long durations of time away from the nest may compromise the aggression defense mechanism. Clearly, however, mother-young reunions of short duration can re-activate the aggression mechanism and exteroceptive cues, to the extent that they are proximate, can maintain the behavior.

As noted earlier (See Figure 5), postpartum aggression is highest at the beginning of the lactation period (around postpartum day 4) and declines to a low level around the time of weaning (post-partum day 21). We became very interested in what role the pups may be playing in the decline in aggression of the mother with advancing lactation (Svare, 1977).

We proposed that the reduction in aggressive behavior by the female might involve the changing stimuli provided by the young as they became older. Thus, we predicted that aggressive behavior would be maintained at high levels in mothers whose maturing young were repeatedly replaced with newborns. Thus, in some mothers, we replaced their young daily with 1–4 day old pups while other mothers did not have their young replaced. We tested the aggressive behavior of the females every 4 days and found that the normal decline in aggressive behavior with advancing lactation was retarded in animals continuously exposed to newborn pups (See Figure 6). Collectively then, these simple experiments were telling us that the offspring were probably playing a very important role in modulating the mothers aggressive behavior during the post-partum period.

7

Determining Where to Go Next

OUR RESEARCH TO THIS point had already uncovered some interesting results regarding this behavior that we were now regularly
referring to as "maternal aggression" or "maternal defense."

It was obvious to us that the behavior was playing a protective
function and was very adaptive to the mother and her young.
Clearly, the offspring were playing a major role in whether or not
and to what extent she would exhibit this kind of intense aggression. Also, it was clear that all she had to do was to sense (see, hear,
smell) the young and not even be in contact with them in order
for the behavior to be maintained once it had been established.
Equally interesting to us however, was the fact that the appearance
of the behavior and then its subsequent decline were related to
dramatic hormonal changes going on within the female as she
went from pregnancy, parturition, lactation, and then the weaning
of her young.

New research ideas were proposed each day and this started to
overwhelm us. It seemed as though many new and interesting
questions were arising with each experiment that we completed.
We had to have some way of categorizing the exciting new ideas in
some logical way so that we could more systematically explore a behavior that we knew so little about. Eventually, we thought that we
could categorize our questions into two broad areas: proximate
causation and ultimate causation.

Questions of proximate causation have to do with the immediate environmental and physiological factors that may influence a

behavior. In the case of maternal aggression, these questions would concern the role of hormones as well as stimuli from the young. These questions would also be concerned with what stimuli from intruding male mice are responsible for provoking the behavior in the female. In other words, what is it about the male that makes the female so threatened, angry, and protective?

In contrast, questions of ultimate causation have to do with the adaptive and evolutionary significance of the behavior. Is this a behavior that has indeed been selected for and has responded to natural selection? Is it possible to demonstrate artificial selection? Does the behavior really function to protect the offspring or is it a byproduct of something else? My research team was discussing these and other questions for significant periods of time each day.

Oftentimes, decisions about research directions have a great deal to do with expertise, previous experience and training, available resources, as well as educated "feelings" about what types of research are more likely to get funded based upon one's background. We sifted through all of these things and soon realized that we had significant strengths in the biology of behavior. Therefore, we felt that the best direction to go in would be to devote most of our efforts toward trying to understand the proximate (immediate) physiological and behavioral factors that were responsible for the behavior. This decision proved to be a good one since we were very productive in our research, were able to answer a good many questions, and we managed to keep getting funded by a number of granting agencies who felt that our research direction was well planned and executed.

Our decision to stick with the biology of behavior also meant that we would have to forsake some research areas. For example, we could not spend time researching issues concerning ultimate causation. Initially we would have to leave that question to others such as evolutionary psychologists and animal behaviorists that were more skilled in doing research in this area. We hoped that scientists specializing in other areas would begin to investigate maternal aggression since it ultimately could help us to answer our own questions. Clearly, when scientists from other disciplines begin to research the same question, they bring fresh viewpoints and new ways of looking at things. However, we felt a great need to stay focused on what we did best instead of becoming distracted. Thus, we stuck with our research plan of investigating the biology of this behavior.

Part III

SEEKING PHYSIOLOGICAL UNDERPINNINGS

8

The Search for a Hormonal Substrate During Pregnancy

OUR INQUIRIES INTO the physiological basis of female aggressive behavior started with an exploration of progesterone involvement in aggression during pregnancy. You will recall that some of our earlier worked showed what appeared to be a close correspondence between the rise of the hormone during pregnancy and the subsequent emergence of threat behavior in the female. We reasoned then that the sudden build up of the hormone might be responsible for elevated levels of threat behavior in pregnant females. We addressed this possibility in several experiments outlined below.

One method for studying progesterone's involvement in the onset of threat behavior during pregnancy is to terminate pregnancy prematurely by what is called hysterectomy (Svare, Miele and Kinsley, 1986). This surgical procedure is very easy to complete while a female is under anesthesia and involves removing both uterine horns with the fetuses still in the horns. The surgical procedure only takes about 10 to 15 minutes to perform and female mice only require a few hours before they have completely recovered. More importantly, progesterone levels rapidly decline, thus providing a technique for exploring what happens to their threat behavior if the hormone suddenly falls.

Our first experiment using this technique compared animals whose pregnancies were terminated on the 15th day of gestation with animals that were sham operated. In the later case, the animals were put under anesthesia, their uterine horns were exposed, but they were not removed. In other words, the sham operated animals were treated identically to the pregnancy-terminated animals with the exception that their pregnancies were allowed to continue. Several days later all the animals were tested for aggression by introducing an adult male mouse to their cage. What we found was that the pregnancy-terminated females no longer exhibited threat behavior while the sham-operated animals continued to exhibit normal aggression. (See Table 4).

Our presumption in the previous experiment was that the reduction in progesterone was the reason why the pregnancy-terminated animals were no longer exhibiting threat behavior. We further tested this hypothesis in another experiment where we pregnancy-terminated (hysterectomized) pregnant females and implanted them with Silastic capsules that would slowly release progesterone into circulation. These implants are easy to make and are implanted just under the skin of the animal where they "make up for" or "replace" the reduction in naturally produced progesterone that the animal would experience from pregnancy termination.

We also included two different control groups in this experiment. One control group of animals were simply pregnancy-terminated and then given a capsule that contained a control substance (sesame oil), which ostensibly has no behavioral or physiological effects. Another control group consisted of pregnant animals that were sham operated and implanted with a control capsule. Our results showed that the pregnancy-terminated female mice that received implants of progesterone were exhibiting aggression that was almost the same as that of animals that were not pregnancy-terminated. Once again, this experiment also seemed to suggest that progesterone could be the key factor in the rise in threat behavior that occurs as a female mouse goes through pregnancy (See Table 4).

TABLE 4. THE RESULTS OF EXPERIMENTS EXAMINING THE EFFECTS OF PREGNANCY TERMINATION ON PREGNANCY-INDUCED AGGRESSION

	Proportion (and %)[b] Fighting	Median (range) Composite aggression score	Number of tests in which fighting was exhibited
Experiment 1[a]			
SHAM	13/14 (93)	5.0 (0.7–11.0)	2.8 (1–3)
HYST	3/15 (20)	*	*
Experiment 2[a]			
SHAM + OIL	17/20 (85)	6.7 (2.0–11.0)	2.9 (1–3)
HYST + 1P	15/20 (75)	3.3 (0.3–8.7)	2.6 (1–3)
HYST + 2P	10/14 (71)	1.4 (0.3–6.3)	1.5 (1–3)
HYST + OIL	1/10 (10)	*	*
Experiment 3[a]			
SHAM + OIL + OIL	16/20 (80)	5.4 (2.7–16.7)	2.3 (1–3)
HYST + P + OIL	16/20 (80)	2.3 (0.3–7.2)	2.7 (1–3)
HYST + P + E	8/20 (40)	0.3 (0.3–2.3)	1.2 (1–3)
HYST + OIL + E	3/20 (15)	*	*
HYST + OIL + OIL	2/20 (10)	*	*

[a]In Experiment 1, aggression was assessed in pregnant female mice that were hysterectomized (HYST) or sham-hysterectomized (SHAM). Experiment 2 explored aggression exhibited by pregnant females that were sham-hysterectomized and implanted with a sesame oil-filled Silastic capsule (SHAM + OIL) or hysterectomized and implanted with oil or one or two progesterone (P)-filled Silastic capsules (HYST + OIL, HYST + 1P, HYST + 2P, respectively). In Experiment 3, aggressive behavior was examined in pregnant mice that were sham-hysterectomized and implanted with two oil capsules (SHAM + OIL + OIL), hysterectomized and implanted with one progesterone (P) and one oil capsule (HYST + P + OIL), hysterectomized and implanted with one P and one estradiol (E) capsule (HYST + P + E), hysterectomized and implanted with one oil and one E capsules (HYST + OIL + E), and hysterectomized and implanted with two oil capsules (HYST + OIL + OIL). In each experiment, surgery was performed on the 15th day of pregnancy with daily aggression tests for 3 days, commencing 24 hr later. Adult male mice, 60–70 days of age, served as opponents.

[b]Exhibiting aggression on at least one test.

*Too few animals fought to report a median.

(From Gandelman and Svare, 1974a, b; Svare, Miele, and Kinsley, 1986)

Another way to explore progesterone involvement in female aggressive behavior is to try to stimulate the behavior in virgin (nonpregnant) female mice by implanting them with progesterone capsules (Mann, Konen, and Svare, 1984). We did this in a series of experiments in which we tested the threat behavior of female mice that were implanted with one or several Silastic capsules filled with progesterone. Additionally, in these experiments, some of the females implanted with progesterone had their ovaries surgically removed (called ovariectomy) while others did not (sham ovariectomy). We did this to control for any possible effects that the female's own endogenous supply of progesterone might have on her behavior. As is typical for experiments of this nature, we also included a

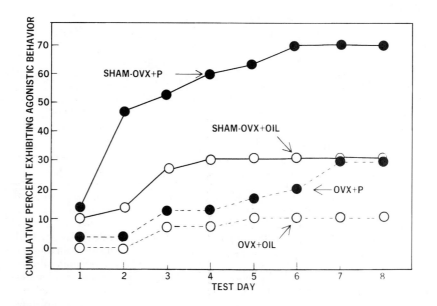

Figure 7. The induction of aggressive behavior in virgin female mice by the administration of progesterone. The figure shows the cumulative percentage of ovariectomized or sham-operated virgin Rockland-Swiss (R-S) females that exhibited aggression toward an R-S male intruder following exposure to a 10-mm capsule containing progesterone (P) or oil. Aggression testing commenced 48 hours following surgery. Subsequent tests were conducted every other day for a maximum of eight tests or until lunging or attacking occurred (Mann, Konen, and Svare, 1984).

TABLE 5. THE AGGRESSIVE BEHAVIOR OF VIRGIN FEMALE MICE WITH OR WITHOUT A PROGESTERONE IMPLANT

	Groups	
Behavioral measures	*Implant intact*	*Implant removed*
Proportion (and %) agonistic (i.e., lunging or attacking) on at least one test	7/12 (58%)	0/12 (0%)**
Median latency (and range) in test days to display agonistic behavior[b]	1.0 (1.0–3.0)	—
Median (and range) number of test days displaying agonistic behavior[b]	2.0 (1.0–3.0)	—
Median (and range) composite score[b]	0.8 (0.5–3.5)	—
Proportion (and %) lunging on at least one test	7/12 (58%)	0/12 (0%)**
Median (and range) number of lunges[b]	0.8 (0.5–2.8)	—
Proportion (and %) attacking on at least one test	2/12 (17%)	0/12 (0%)
Median (and range) number of attacks	[c]	—

[a]Adult Rockland-Swiss (R-S) female mice were subcutaneously implanted with a 10-man Silastic capsule containing progesterone (P). Two weeks following P treatment, their aggressive behavior toward an adult R-S male was assessed during a single 5-min test. Those females that exhibited aggressive behavior were anesthetized and the implant was either removed (Group Implant Removed) or left in place (Group Implant Intact). Forty-eight hours later the females were retested every other day for a total of four tests.

[b]Of those animals exhibiting the behavior.

[c]Too few animals exhibited the behavior to permit calculation of the median.

**Significantly different from females with implants intact, $P < 0.003$.

(From Mann, Konen, and Svare, 1984)

control group of virgin females that received implants of sesame oil. Our results showed that females receiving progesterone implants exhibited elevations in threat behaviors but only if they had their ovaries (See Figure 7).

In another experiment in this line of work, we also showed that threat behaviors would decrease once the progesterone capsules were removed from the females. Also, in other experiments, we were able to show that the threat behavior of virgin females treated with progesterone was similar, though not identical to that of normal pregnant female mice (See Table 5).

This work gave further credibility to the idea that progesterone may be playing an important role in the aggression observed during pregnancy but it also suggested that some other hormone from the ovaries, perhaps estrogen, might also be important. None-the-less we felt confident at this point that progesterone was the key player in what we were now calling "pregnancy-induced" aggres-sion and we were ready to begin to move on and look at other stages of the behavior during the early postpartum period and lac-tation. Before moving on to that other research however, it is im-portant that you not get the impression that everything could be neatly packaged at this point and there simply were no additional questions to ask about pregnancy-induced aggression. This clearly is not the case.

9

Additional Questions and Shades of Gray Regarding Pregnancy-Induced Aggression

OUR RESEARCH ON progesterone's involvement in pregnancy-induced aggression showed that the hormone did not fully induce threat behavior in virgin females that was identical to that of normal pregnant animals. Estrogen, we thought, was also playing a role since only virgin females that had their ovaries could be stimulated to show threat behaviors following chronic progesterone exposure.

We conducted other experiments in which we explored different combinations of progesterone with estrogen and generally we found that these treatments were not successful in fully duplicating the threat behavior of normal pregnant animals. Additionally, estrogen in some of the experiments actually seemed to be inhibiting aggression (See Table 4). This is still perplexing to us since it indicates that the relationships between progesterone and perhaps other hormones may be much more complex than we thought.

We also thought about the possible involvement of other hormones during pregnancy. Progesterone was selected only because it was the most obvious since it had been implicated in other aspects of maternal behavior in rodents (like nestbuilding for example) and was known to be changing so dramatically. Clearly, there are other reproductive hormones like the adrenal hormones (corticosterone) or pituitary hormones like oxytocin, prolactin, and adrenocorticotrophic hormone and a myriad of others that have been implicated in other behaviors.

Members of my research group also became interested in studying where in the brain progesterone might be acting to promote aggression. Those studying the biological basis of other reproductive behaviors like sex and maternal behavior had shown that progesterone seems to act in the hypothalamus of the brain This is a part of what is called the old brain or the limbic system. It would be interesting we thought to explore if this area of the brain also mediates pregnancy-induced aggression. Thus, the more research we were doing, the more interesting questions were surfacing.

As you can see, to continue to research all of these possibilities would take many more experiments and even greater time and resource investment. They are interesting questions but ones that we did not feel as much urgency to address as others. Interestingly, some of these research topics are currently being explored in our laboratory but also in other laboratories that have become interested in the topic. The scientific community has a way of picking up on interesting phenomena and spreading the word so to speak about research problems requiring additional study.

10

Searching for a Biological Substrate for Postpartum Docility

ONCE FEMALE MICE GO through pregnancy and deliver their offspring, they enter a brief period where they exhibit very little aggressive behavior toward a male intruder. This period, which lasts from 24 to 48 hours following parturition, is a time in which female mice ordinarily are highly sexually receptive and will mate with a male mouse instead of responding aggressively. This period is referred to as postpartum estrous and corresponds to a time when progesterone has fallen off very sharply and estrogen has momentarily increased.

Postpartum estrous and the hormone changes responsible for it (declining progesterone and rising estrogen) is observed in many female mammals, including humans, shortly after delivering their offspring (See Figure 5). Many experiments in behavioral endocrinology laboratories have documented the importance of estrogen for stimulating female sexual behavior. In light of this information then, we next focused our attention on pinpointing the physiological reasons responsible for the transition from threat behavior during pregnancy to docile behavior during the immediate postpartum period. Since the hormone coming from the ovaries, estrogen, seemed to be such a logical candidate we conducted several experiments to explore its possible role.

In one experiment (Ghiraldi, Plonsky, and Svare, 1994), we

ovariectomized (surgically removed the ovaries) of pregnant female mice shortly before they delivered their young on the 18th
day of gestation. Once the animals delivered their young, they
were tested for their reaction toward an intruder male that was
placed in their cage. This was done on the day they delivered as
well as each subsequent day for a total of 4 tests. A separate group
of female mice was sham-operated on the 18th day of pregnancy
and otherwise was treated and tested for aggression in an identical manner.

We found that animals without ovaries exhibited an accelerated
onset of aggression in that they started to exhibit attacking behavior (postpartum aggression) shortly after they delivered their
young. In contrast, the sham operated animals did not begin to exhibit aggression until 48 to 72 hours following the delivery of their
offspring (See Figure 8).

The findings outlined above suggested to us that the absence of
aggression normally seen immediately following the delivery of
young was probably related to the postpartum estrous surge of estrogen that occurs at that time. Our ovariectomy procedure was apparently preventing that surge and therefore aggressive behavior instead of docile behavior was turned on in the absence of estrogen.

To make our conclusion regarding estrogen more definitive, we
conducted another experiment in which we administered subcu-
taneous injections of the hormone estrogen to pregnant female
mice that had been ovariectomized on the 18th day of pregnancy.
We then compared the onset of aggression in these animals with
those that were ovariectomized but were instead administered the
control substance sesame oil.

Consistent with our previous results, we found that the estrogen treated animals performed like animals that had their ovaries;
namely, they did not begin to show aggression until 24 to 48 hours
following the delivery of young. In contrast, animals that were
ovariectomized and injected with sesame oil showed the accelerated onset of aggression (See Figure 9).

Taken together, these experiments clearly demonstrated that
the normal role of estrogen just after parturition is probably to suppress aggression so that females can mate with a male and therefore further enhance their reproductive fitness.

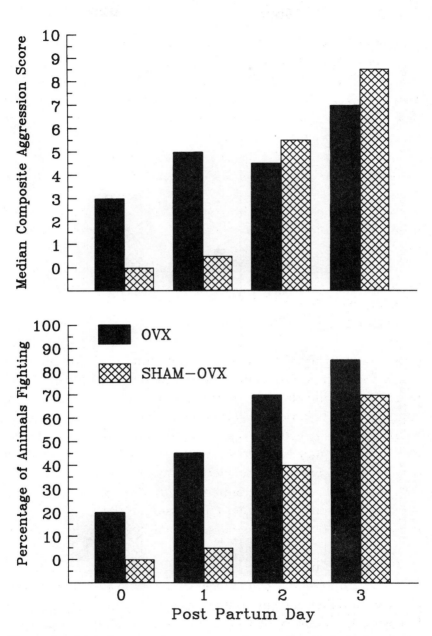

Figure 8. The influence of ovary removal on aggressive behavior during the early postpartum period. The figure shows the incidence (bottom) and median intensity (top) of postpartum aggression displayed by females that were ovariectomized (OVX) or sham-operated (SHAM-OVX) on Gestation Day 18 as a function of postpartum test day (Ghiraldi, Plonsky and Svare, 1993).

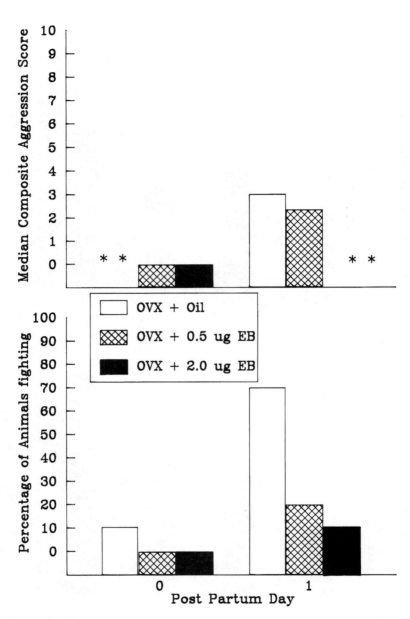

Figure 9. The influence of estrogen injections on aggressive behavior of ovariectomized mice during the early postpartum period. The figure shows the incidence (bottom) and median intensity (top) of postpartum aggression displayed by ovariectomized females treated with 0.5 or 2.0 µg estradiol benzoate (EB) dissolved in 0.05 cc sesame oil (OVX + 0.5 µg EB, and OVX + 2.0 µg EB, respectively), or oil vehicle alone (OVX + Oil) as a function of postpartum test day (**Indicates too few cases to compute a median). (Ghiraldi, Plonsky, and Svare, 1993)

   Once again, we were at a point where we could pursue some very interesting findings as well as address other issues of proximate causality. For example, we could spend considerable time and resources exploring just how estrogen inhibits aggression. Our research team began proposing a number of experiments to look at just where in the brain estrogen might be acting to suppress aggression. However, others in our group were more interested in understanding how aggression gets switched on after the second or third day following the delivery of young. This seemed like a much more interesting and fruitful avenue of research. Afterall, what had initially captivated our attention was the dramatic and intense attacking behavior that females showed once they had nursed their pups for a few days after delivery. Thus, once again, we would leave to others the task of further exploring the mechanisms responsible for postpartum docility shortly following the delivery of young.

11

Searching for the Biological Underpinnings of Postpartum Aggression

YOU WILL RECALL from some of our previous research that female mice become intensely aggressive after they have been with their offspring for about 48 to 72 hours. We reasoned that the stimuli provided by the offspring were of great importance to the subsequent rise in maternal or postpartum aggressive behavior in the female.

One stimulus provided by the young that is particularly crucial for their growth is that of suckling stimulation. When a mother mouse nurses her young, the pups attach to her nipples and suck vigorously causing the formation and secretion of milk (See Figure 10). We reasoned that if we eliminated this stimulus, postpartum female mice probably would never begin to develop maternal defense.

In a series of experiments (Svare and Gandelman, 1976) we performed a very simple surgical procedure on pregnant female mice in which we removed their nipples (called thelectomy), therefore preventing them from receiving suckling stimulation from their young once they delivered. Even though these females exhibited perfectly normal maternal behavior and even assumed a nursing posture over their young following parturition, we found that they

Figure 10. A lactating Rockland-Swiss (R-S) albino mouse nursing her 6 day old young. Note the posturing of the mother, which allows the young to suckle from her teats.

never developed aggressive behavior. Because they could not provide milk to their offspring and therefore the young would die, the females were given new (recently suckled) newborn pups every day to ensure that they were exposed to vigorous pup stimulation at all times. Even with this procedure, the thelectomized mothers never developed aggressive behavior (See Table 6).

We began to think that the critical stimulus for the initiation of aggressive behavior after the mother delivered her young was the suckling stimulation she received from her pups during nursing. Indeed, a whole independent set of observations in some other experiments was leading us in exactly the same direction.

We were conducting experiments in which we would give newborn mouse pups to virgin female mice to see whether or not we could induce them to begin displaying aggressive behavior. Our logic in these "induction" experiments was very simple: We thought that the presence of the pups alone might be enough to stimulate aggression in a mouse that has never gone through preg-

**TABLE 6. THE RESULTS OF EXPERIMENTS EXAMINING
THE INFLUENCE OF NIPPLE REMOVAL ON
POSTPARTUM AGGRESSION.**

Time of Thelectomy	Group	Proportion and Percentage of Animals Fighting On At Least 1 of 8 Days	Average Number of Tests In Which Fighting Was Observed**	Presence or Absence of Milk In Mammary Glands
Prior to mating	Sham-P	17/24 (71%)	6.2	+
	Thel-P	4/24 (17%)	3.8	0
	Sham-NP	0/24 (0%)	—	0
Day 18 of pregnancy	Sham-P	15/24 (63%)	6.3	+
	Thel-P	3/24 (13%)	6.0	0
Postpartum Day 5 (First test - Postpartum Day 6)	Sham-P	12/24 (50%)	7.3	+
	Thel-P	13/24 (54%)	6.3	0
Postpartum Day 5 (First test - Postpartum Day 12)	Sham-P	14/24 (63%)*	3.6	+
	Thel-P	17/24 (71%)	3.6	0
Immediate post-partum interval	Sham-24-P	15/24 (63%)	7.0	+
	Thel-48-P	15/24 (63%)	6.5	0
	Thel-24-P	6/24 (25%)	6.0	0

The behavior of thelectomized mice fostered young (Thel-P) and sham-thelectomized mice fostered (Sham-P) and not fostered (Sham-NP) young toward adult males. In the last experiment thelectomy and the fostering of young occurred either 24 (Thel-24-P) or 48 hr (Thel-48-P) following parturition. Sham operations were performed 24 hr following parturition (Sham-24-P).

*Only received 4 aggression tests.

**Based only upon those animals that fought.

(From Svare and Gandelman, 1976b)

nancy and delivered offspring. In other words, perhaps the presence of pups is a sufficient factor in turning on aggressive behavior in a female mouse.

The logic stated above was only partially correct and we went through a phase in our work in which we had repeated failures. The experiments consisted of the following procedure: We would foster newborn pups to virgin female mice every day for several months and periodically test the female for her aggressive behavior by placing a male mouse in her cage for a short test. The virgin female mice would respond in a maternal fashion to the foster pups by retrieving, licking them, and hovering over them in a nursing posture. However, they could not nurse the young and give milk to them since their nipples (teats) and mammary glands were not developed.

The development of the mammary glands and teats is something that only happens during pregnancy and since these virgin female mice had never gone through this reproductive state, they were incapable of performing this biological function. Therefore, each day we would take out the foster young in the cage and replace them with new foster young. The pups would be left with the mother for 24 hours and then "fresh" (recently suckled pups from another mother) would be given to her. This procedure was repeated daily, sometimes for months on end.

Even though the females were exhibiting normal maternal care and were even hovering over the pups in a nursing posture that is common for the female mouse, none of the animals would exhibit any aggressive behavior toward a male when it was introduced to the cage. Try as we might (we spent nearly 3 years on these experiments!), we simply could not get these virgin females to show postpartum aggression by giving them extended pup stimulation.

Just as we were completing the induction experiments, our thelectomy findings were showing the importance of suckling stimulation for the development of aggression in postpartum females after they had delivered their offspring. Based on those experiments then, we reasoned that virgin female mice could not be induced to show aggression simply because they lacked the nipple growth that normally occurs during pregnancy. Hence, without this growth, they could not receive suckling and therefore they would never become aggressive. Put another way, virgin females were acting just like the thelectomized females in the previously mentioned experiment—no nipples = no suckling = no aggression.

We found that the nipples in mice grow very dramatically during pregnancy (Svare, Mann and Samuels, 1980) (See Figure 11). Indeed there is a threefold increase in the length of the nipples

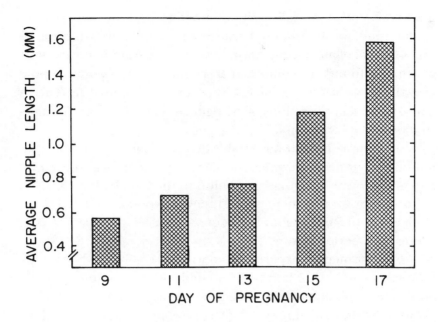

Figure 11. The growth of nipples during pregnany. The figure shows the mean nipple length of pregnant female R-S mice as a function of time of gestation. Separate groups of pregnant animals were sacrificed on Days 9, 11, 13, 15, or 17 of gestation and their nipples were removed and measured with dial calipers under a dissecting microscope. Because nipple position did not influence nipple length, the data for each animal represents the average of 10 nipples (Svare, Mann, and Samuels, 1980).

during pregnancy. With this in mind, we reasoned that if we "grew" nipples in virgin female mice and then gave them suckling stimulation from mouse pups, we could finally induce aggression in these mice comparable to that of females that had gone through pregnancy and delivered their own offspring. All of this sounded simple, but proved very difficult since we had no idea how to grow nipples in mice.

After reading a number of endocrinology and reproductive physiology books, our research group arrived at the conclusion that a wide variety of hormones were involved in the growth of the mammary glands and nipples in mammals. Growth hormone, corticosterone, estrogen, progesterone, and prolactin were mentioned most frequently especially as it pertained to cows and sheep. With this in mind, we spent several years exploring the growth promoting potential of all of these hormones in mice. After many failures, we finally found a regimen that produced substantial nipple growth in virgin female mice (Svare and Gandelman, 1976a). It consisted of daily injections of estrogen and progesterone for a period of 18 days (See Table 7).

Once nipple growth was established in virgin female mice, we reasoned that newborn pups should be able to attach to the nipples and provide suckling stimulation to the female. If suckling is so critical for aggression to occur, then we hypothesized that these females should begin showing aggression after they had nursed young for a period of time.

We performed an experiment in which we gave newborn pups to virgin females that had been treated with the nipple growing hormone combination. We tested the animals for aggression just prior to the time that they were given newborns and on several occasions after they had been exposed to newborns. Once again, we used a fostering procedure in which the virgin females were given new offspring every 24 hours so as to ensure that they would receive vigorous suckling stimulation at all times.

TABLE 7. NIPPLE GROWTH RESULTING FROM ESTROGEN AND PROGESTERONE INJECTIONS.

Group	N	Average Nipple Length (mm)	Average Nipple Base Diameter (mm)
Pregnant	6	1.40** ± 0.05	0.66** ± 0.06
OVX + EB + P	6	0.99* ± 0.07	0.55* ± 0.14
OVX + OIL	6	0.49 ± 0.08	0.41 ± 0.08
S-OVX + OIL	6	0.47 ± 0.13	0.41 ± 0.06

The average nipple length and base diameter of a representative nipple (second right thoracic) for pregnant mice (Pregnant), ovariectomized virgin mice treated with estradiol benzoate and progesterone to induce nipple growth (OVX + EB + P), ovariectomized and treated with oil (OVX + OIL), or sham-ovariectomized and given oil (S-OVX + OIL). Nipples were removed and measured on the 19th day of pregnancy or following 19 days of steroid or oil treatment.

*Significantly different from Group OVX + OIL and S-OVX + OIL.

**Significantly different from Group OVX + EB + P.

(From Svare and Gandelman, 1976a)

What we found was that these females did in fact suckle their young. When we picked up the virgin females by the tail, the pups were attached to the nipples; also the nipples were very red and distended from having been suckled by the pups. More importantly, we also found that these virgin females now exhibited aggressive behavior almost identical to that of females that had gone through pregnancy, delivery (parturition), and were nursing their young (Svare and Gandelman, 1976a). While they would exhibit some threat behaviors prior to receiving suckling stimulation from pups, they exhibited the full blown, intense postpartum-like aggression after they received a few days of suckling from newborns.

In additional experiments (Svare and Gandelman, 1976a) we also found that these "induced" virgin females responded to nipple removal (thelectomy) in the same way that normal pregnant mice did. That is to say, they would not develop aggressive behavior once they were exposed to newborns since they could not receive suckling stimulation from them. (See Table 8).

A number of findings were beginning to make sense at this point in our research program. However, none were more critical than the fact that suckling simulation seemed to be so important for turning on aggression once females had delivered their young. Suckling in mammals (humans included) is absolutely critical to the process called lactation. When newborns suckle from their mother, they cause the hypothalamus and the pituitary gland to secrete hormones like prolactin, oxytocin, growth hormone, and adrenocorticotrophic hormone (ACTH) to name a few. This is called the "neuroendocrine reflex arc" and it is critical to the production and secretion of milk from the mammary glands (See Figure 12).

Could it be that the hormones that are so critical to milk formation and secretion are also involved in "turning on" aggression in the female once she delivers her offspring and receives a few days of suckling stimulation from them? This question is one that has occupied an enormous amount of our time and energy through the years.

One hormone that repeatedly has been implicated in maternal behavior in mammals is prolactin. This hormone does seem to work on some very specific brain areas to regulate maternal behaviors

**TABLE 8. THE AGGRESSIVE BEHAVIOR OF VIRGIN FEMALE
MICE TREATED WITH HORMONES (EXPERIMENT 1)
OR THELECTOMIZED (EXPERIMENT 2).**

Group	n	Number fighting before presenting foster young	Proportion (and %) of animals fighting after pup exposure	Latency to begin fighting after pup exposure (d)	Average number of fights*^
Experiment 1					
Parturient	22	0	12/22 (54)	1.8 ± 0.8	—
OVX + EB + P	24	0	12/24 (50)	1.3 ± 0.6	—
OVX + Oil	20	0	1/20 (05)	1.0	—
S-OVX + Oil	19	0	1/19 (05)	2.0	—
Experiment 2					
Parturient + THEL	20	0	4/20 (20)	1.3 ± 0.4	9.8 ± 0.4
Parturient + S + THEL	20	0	13/20 (65)	1.6 ± 1.1	8.6 ± 2.1
OVX + EB + P + THEL	20	0	2/20 (10)	2.5 ± 1.5	8.0 ± 1.0
OVX + EB + P + S-THEL	20	0	12/20 (60)	2.1 ± 2.4	8.2 ± 2.5

* Animals in Experiment 1 were killed after they fought in two successive tests.

^ Animals in Experiment 2 were given 10 aggression tests. The data are derived from only the animals that fought.

Experiment 1: Aggressive behavior of RS female mice that were either mated (parturient), ovariectomised and primed with oestradiol benzoate and progesterone to induce nipple growth (OVX + EB + P), ovariectomised and treated with oil (OVX + Oil), or sham ovariectomised and given oil (S-OVX + Oil). Aggressive behavior was scored before exposure to pups (on the last day of hormone or oil treatment or on day 19 of gestation) and on each succeeding day for 10 days after presentation of foster young or until fights were displayed on 2 successive days.

Experiment 2: Aggressive behavior of RS females that were mated and either thelectomised (parturient + THEL) or sham thelectomised on day 19 of pregnancy (parturient + S + THEL) and of ovariectomised hormone-treated mice either thelectomised (OVX + EB + P + THEL) or sham thelectomised (OVX + EB + P + S-THEL) on the day after the last hormone injections.

(From Svare and Gandelman, 1976a)

like pup retrieval and nestbuilding. Indeed, in many research publications in the area of reproductive physiology it has actually been called the "maternal" hormone. We felt then that a logical place to begin exploring hormonal involvement in postpartum aggression would be prolactin.

Ergot drugs are chemicals that have been developed to suppress the formation and secretion of prolactin from the pituitary gland. When injected into female mammals they are know to cause

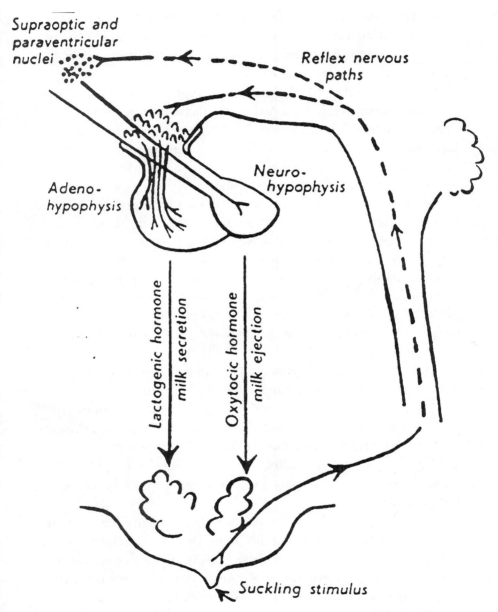

Figure 12. The neuroendocrine reflex arc. The figure shows the probable neurohormonal reflexes involved in milk secretion and milk ejection. (From Harris. G.W.: Neural Control of the Pituitary Gland. London, Edward Arnold Publishers, 1955).

a relatively rapid reduction in circulating levels of this hormone by working as dopamine agonists. That is to say, they promote the release of the important brain neurotransmitter dopamine, which in turn suppresses prolactin release.

We explored the effectiveness of two ergot drugs, ergocornine and bromocryptine, in suppressing prolactin and postpartum aggression. Female mice that had just delivered their offspring were injected daily with one of these drugs or a control substance. Each day the animals were given new offspring in order to maintain high and vigorous rates of suckling stimulation.

Figure 13 shows the suppressive effects that ergot drugs have upon lactation in the postpartum mouse (Mann, Michael, and Svare, 1980). Lactation was assessed by measuring weight gain in pups every day. A mother mouse whose prolactin secretion is normal will easily secrete milk to her young while nursing them. Weight gain of the young therefore is a good indirect reflection of prolactin secretion. As can be seen from Figure 13, the ergot drugs were suppressing lactation most likely as a consequence of reduced prolactin secretion.

Table 9 shows the effects of ergot drugs on circulating prolactin levels and on the aggressive behavior of postpartum mice. It is interesting to note that the drugs dramatically reduced (but did not fully eliminate) prolactin levels in the blood but left aggression unimpaired. Ergot treated postpartum females were as aggressive as control subjects. This finding therefore suggested to us that prolactin probably does not play a role in the aggressive behavior of postpartum mice.

It is important to note here that we needed to involve a collaborator at another institution at this point. Dr. Sandy Michael, an endocrinologist at SUNY-Binghamtom, is one of the few people in the world that can perform assays of mouse prolactin. We therefore shipped to her samples of blood taken from the mice used in this experiment as well as other experiments so that she could perform the needed biochemical assays. Her involvement in this work became essential to the continued success of our research program.

An alternate explanation for our ergot drug experiments

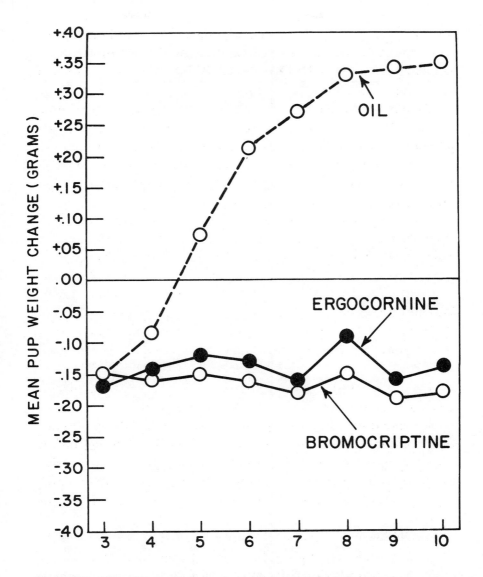

Figure 13. The effects of prolactin inhibitors on lactation in the mouse. The figure shows the mean pup weight gain per day for young nursed by parturient females treated daily from Postpartum Days 1-10 with oil , 0.5 mg of ergocornine, or 0.5 mg bromocryptine. Five 1 to 4-day-old pups were fostered beginning on Postpartum Day 3. They were weighed and exchanged daily for five pre-weighed replete pups through Postpartum Day 10 (Mann, Michael, and Svare, 1980).

TABLE 9. THE INFLUENCE OF PROLACTIN INHIBITORS ON POSTPARTUM AGGRESSION.

Group	Oil	Ergocornine	Bromocryptine
Aggression			
Proportion (and %) fighting	8/12 (67)	6/11 (55)	8/13 (62)
Latency (in test days) to exhibit aggression [b,c]	1.6 (± .2)	1.5 (± 7)	1.8 (± .5)
Number of tests in which fighting occurred [b,c]	3.4 (± .7)	3.0 (± .6)	2.6 (± .5)
Number of attacks [b,c]	3.6 (± .8)	5.0 (± 1.7)	3.8 (± 2.0)
Suckling			
Proportion (and %) receiving suckling	12/12 (100)	11/11 (100)	3/13 (100)
Lactation			
Proportion (and %) lactating	12/12 (100)	1/11 (09)	0/13 (00)
Plasma prolactin (ng/ml)[b]			
All animals	152.0 (± 21.4)	22.8 (± 7.1)	73.9 (± 23.1)
Fighters	143.3 (± 31.8)	22.6 (± 11.8)	81.1 (± 33.0)
Nonfighters	173.4 (± 22.4)	23.2 (± 6.6)	62.5 (± 40.0)
Correlations (rho)[c]			
Plasma PRL versus			
Latency (in test days) to exhibit aggression	−0.18	+ 0.42	−0.17
Number of tests in which fighting occurred	+ 0.18	−0.05	−0.37
Number of attacks	+ 0.44	−0.17	−0.56

Parturient R-S mice were treated daily from Postpartum Days 1–10 with oil, 0.5 mg ergocornine, or 0.5 mg bromocryptine. Five 1- to 4-day old pups were fostered beginning on Postpartum Day 3. They were weighed and exchanged daily for five preweighed replete pups through Postpartum Day 10. Three-minute tests for aggression against an adult male intruder were conducted on Postpartum Days 4, 6, 8, and 10. On Postpartum Day 11, blood samples were withdrawn from the dams by cardiac puncture without anesthesia and plasma prolactin (PRL) analyzed.

[b]Mean ± SEM

[c]Of those animals that fought.

(From Svare, Mann, and Samuels, 1980)

concerned the fact that we had not completely eliminated the secretion of prolactin and that some of the hormone was still getting into circulation and, hence, may have been enough to activate aggressive behavior. We reasoned that a better procedure for eliminating prolactin from circulation in contrast to drug treatment would be to perform what is called a surgical hypophysectomy (Svare, Mann, Broida, and Michael, 1982).

This manipulation detaches and removes the pituitary gland from the hypothalamus and eliminates the production and release of prolactin as well as other pituitary hormones such as oxytocin, growth hormone and ACTH. To perform this experiment, we surgically removed the pituitary gland from female mice right after they delivered their young and before they received any suckling stimulation. After surgery, we gave them fresh newborn pups every 24 hours to maintain high rates of suckling and we assessed their aggressive behavior by placing a male in their cage for a brief period of time each day. We also included two control groups of animals: one that received a sham operation (they were treated identically except the pituitary gland was not removed) and one that was not operated on at all (this is called a non-operated control). Like our experiments with the ergot drugs, we also assessed in every animal the level of prolactin in circulation.

Table 10 shows that hypophysectomy eliminated prolactin release. Levels of the hormone in animals without a pituitary gland were at what is called non-specific binding levels, which essentially means there is no hormone present. In spite of the fact that the hypophysectomized animals were rendered prolactin deficient (indeed pituitary hormone deficient!), they continued to try and nurse their young. Even though they could not lactate, they received suckling stimulation and, most importantly, they exhibited perfectly normal levels of aggressive behavior.

The results of the prolactin experiments described here were counterintuitive to us. Wasn't prolactin supposed to be the so-called maternal hormone? If not prolactin, how about the other pituitary hormones like oxytocin for example? Apparently, our hypophysectomy findings clearly demonstrated that no pituitary hormone was

TABLE 10. THE AGGRESSIVE BEHAVIOR AND PROLACTIN LEVELS
OF HYPOPHYSECTOMIZED POSTPARTUM MICE

Group	Proportion (and %) fighting on at least one test	Mean (±SEM) latency (in test days) to exhibit fighting[a]	Mean (±SEM) number of tests fighting[a]	Mean (±SEM) number of attacks[a]	Mean (±SEM) plasma prolactin (ng/ml) levels
NOC	14/24 (0.58)	2.6 ± 0.3	2.3 ± 0.3	2.6 ± 0.6	159.4 ± 46.2
SHAM	19/32 (0.59)	2.3 ± 0.3	2.7 ± 0.3	3.9 ± 0.5	124.5 ± 28.6
HYPOX	15/22 (0.68)	1.7 ± 0.2	2.8 ± 0.3	2.9 ± 0.5	5.3 ± 1.3

[a]Only for those animals exhibiting aggression

Maternal aggressive behavior and plasma prolactin (PRL) levels of parturient Rockland-Swiss albino female mice that were hypophysectomized (HYPOX), Sham-Operated (SHAM), or Nonoperated (NOC)

(From Svare, Mann, Broida, and Michael, 1982)

involved so now what? What was suckling doing to the female mouse to make her so aggressive?

An intermediary step between suckling stimulation and the ultimate secretion of hormones from the pituitary gland is the rapid change in the production (called turnover) of various neurotransmitters in the hypothalamus. These neurotransmitter changes are known to be involved in the production and release of hormones from the pituitary gland. Hypothalamic turnover rates of the neurotransmitter serotonin dramatically increase once a female begins to receive suckling from her young while she is nursing.

Reproductive physiologists have shown that the neural system from the nipples goes through the spinothalamic tracts and ultimately terminates in the hypothalamus of the brain. In the hypothalamus, neurotransmitter functioning (usually referred to as synthesis and turnover rates) changes directly as a result of the frequency and the intensity of suckling stimulation that a mother mouse receives. More importantly, however, psychobiologists and psychiatrists have known for quite some time that the neurotransmitter serotonin has been implicated in many types of violent and aggressive behaviors in humans and lower animals. Perhaps, we reasoned, aggression in the female mouse is turned on when suckling activates the serotonergic system in the hypothalamus. This hypothesis then became the next one for us to vigorously pursue.

By turning our research program into the area of psychopharmacology and away from hormones, we were about to enter new and challenging territory. It was necessary for us to become more educated than we were regarding neurotransmitter function and basic pharmacology. Thus, we spent considerable time just learning about different drugs and how and where they worked in the brain. It was a whole new world in many respects and caused us to perform some relatively inept experiments at times.

After going down many blind paths, we finally started having some success when we began using drugs that were specific serotonin depletors (called PCPA) or specific serotonin receptor blockers (methysergide). The results of one such experiment are shown in Figure 14. Postpartum mice were administered one of these drugs and then tested for aggression 45 to 90 minutes following drug

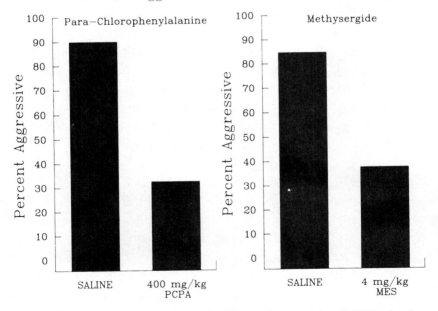

Figure 14. The pharmacological effects of serotonin (5-HT) altering drugs on the postpartum aggressive behavior of mice. Lactating females on Postpartum Day 6 were tested for aggressive behavior toward a male 90 minutes after receiving 400 mg/kg of PCPA or 45 minutes following 4 mg/kg methysergide (Svare, 1989).

administration. These two drugs dramatically reduced aggressive behavior in postpartum females presumably as a consequence of the serotonin altering effects that they produced in specific areas of the hypothalamus (Svare, 1989).

The fact that we were able to change postpartum aggressive behavior by changing the serotonergic system would seem to provide closure on just what biological mechanism is essential for this interesting behavior. However, ongoing research in our laboratory suggests that the picture is much more complex since we have begun to implicate another chemical system, the endogenous opioids, in female aggression. The early stages of this work suggests that a complex interaction between the opioids and serotonin ultimately may provide the key to understanding why female mice become so aggressive once they have received suckling stimulation from their young.

Part IV

UNDERSTANDING INDIVIDUAL VARIATION

12

Why Study Individual Differences?

IN ADDITION TO exploring the hormonal mechanisms underlying pregnancy-induced and postpartum aggression, we were also starting to examine the mechanisms underlying individual variation in these aggressive behaviors. Understanding individual differences in behavior was one of the original goals of psychology as it evolved as a discipline many years ago. The reasoning has always been that unlocking the keys to such differences can help us to understand fundamental principles that control behavioral responses. Indeed, in my own subspecialty of psychology, behavioral endocrinology, we have always sought to understand why animals exhibit such tremendous variability in behavioral responses.

In our own research, that of female aggressive behavior during pregnancy and lactation, we repeatedly had found that our Rockland-Swiss outbred mice that were not treated experimentally in any way showed very dramatic individual variation in aggression. You probably noticed this in many of the figures and tables that are included in this book.

In the case of aggression displayed during pregnancy, some animals exhibited no threat behavior at all (roughly 20-40%) while others exhibited lunges and yet others exhibited both lunges and intense biting attacks! Similarly, in the case of aggression observed during the postpartum period, some mothers were intensely aggressive, exhibiting as many as 20 biting attacks toward a male in a 3 minute test, while other animals exhibited only 1 or 2 attacks.

Indeed, other postpartum females (roughly 20–40%) exhibited no aggression at all!

In searching for the possible biological underpinnings of these individual differences, we focused on hormones and neurotransmitters as possible determinants. For example, in one study we explored whether or not individual variation in pregnancy-induced aggression was related to circulating levels of progesterone (Mann, Konen, and Svare, 1984). You will recall from the work reviewed previously that this hormone has been shown to be very important for stimulating the aggression observed during pregnancy.

If progesterone is important in modulating individual differences in pregnancy-induced aggression, then one might expect to see very high levels of progesterone in very aggressive pregnant mice and very low levels of the hormone in animals that are not aggressive or that exhibit low levels of the behavior. When we did perform this kind of an experiment (See Figure 15) we found that there was absolutely no relationship of any kind between individual variation in the behavior and circulating levels of progesterone. Similar work was also done with prolactin and postpartum aggression but this also failed to show a relationship between levels of the behavior and levels of the hormone (Broida, Michael, and Svare, 1981). We currently are exploring whether or not individual variation in serotonergic function (synthesis, level, or turnover) might be related to individual differences in postpartum aggression.

Our failure to relate individual differences in aggressive behavior to variation in circulating levels of hormones did not deter us from examining other important factors that might contribute to such variation. For example, some of our work has shown that an animal's genetic background may be very important in determining

---

Figure 15. (*facing page*) The relationship between progesterone and pregnancy-induced aggression in the mouse. The figure shows the incidence and intensity of agonistic behaviors and median levels of plasma progesterone (P) of pregnant Rockland Swiss (R-S) female mice as a function of gestation day. Separate groups of animals were given a single 5-minute aggression test against an adult R-S male intruder on Gestation Day 6, 10, 14, or 18. The percentage of animals displaying the behavior

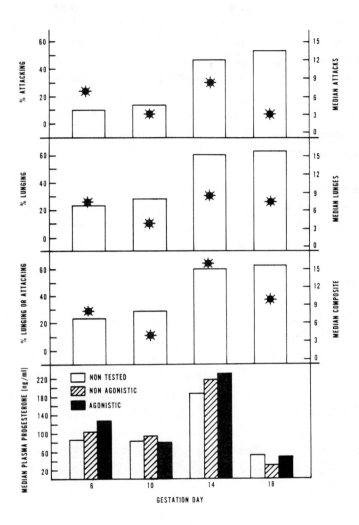

is represented by histograms and median intensity scores are depicted by asterisks. Within 5 minutes of the behavioral test, blood was obtained by cardiac puncture for radioimmunoassay of circulating P. In order to examine the effects of behavioral testing on P levels, additional groups of animals were not behaviorally tested and were blood sampled for determination of plasma P. For comparison purposes, median P levels of non-tested, non-agonistic, and agonistic females as a function of the day of gestation are shown in the bottom panel (Mann, Konen, and Svare, 1984).

whether or not and to what extent it will become aggressive during pregnancy and lactation. Still other research from our laboratory shows that a female's prior intrauterine position (i.e., the position that it occupies in its mother's womb when it is just a fetus!) also influences how much aggression she will exhibit when she is pregnant and lactating. These effects are called developmental effects since they occur at very early ages and influence behavioral responses at points distant from when they exert their primary biological effects.

13

The Important Role of Genes in Shaping Individual Variation in Aggression

ONE WAY TO EXPLORE whether or not genes influence a particular behavior is to work with mice that are classified as inbred. In any strain of inbred mice, the animals have been maintained through many generations of brother-sister matings. What happens then is that these animals are genetically identical to one another. For example, if you take any two females from a particular inbred strain, their degree of genetic similarity is around 99.999%! In humans, the development of two genetically identical twins occurs when one fertilized ova divides therefore creating two separate but identical beings. Inbred mice therefore are like having many identical twins at one's disposal. The added advantage with mice however is that all animals of the strain are identical instead of just a few pairs of identical twins.

All of our previous work had employed random bred albino mice which resulted in heterozygous genetic backgrounds (i.e., mice whose genetic backgrounds were highly variable). To the extent that genes regulate maternal aggression then, one would expect to see lots of individual variation in behavior since there was lots of individual variation in genotype. Thus, comparing the aggressive behavior of female inbred mice that represented radically different genetic makeups, could help determine to what extent genes actually regulate individual variation in female aggression.

In this work we utilized two inbred mouse strains, the C57BL/6J and DBA/2J. These inbred strains are among the most popular used in biomedical research since a great deal is known about their physiology and behavior. We found that DBA/2J mice exhibit relatively high levels of both pregnancy-induced and postpartum aggression in comparison to C57BL/6J animals (Broida and Svare, 1982; Svare, 1988) (See Tables 11 and 12).

We also found that nothing could really modify this strain difference. In one experiment, we gave the animals additional reproductive experience by mating females several times and looking at their aggression during each pregnancy and lactation period. We found that it did not lower the aggression of the DBA females or alternatively increase the aggression of C57BL animals—the strain difference remained the same (See Table 12).

Also, if we cross-fostered animals in which we allowed DBA mothers to rear C57BL females and vice versa it had no impact upon their aggression. The females always behaved true to their genotype with C57BL females exhibiting very low levels of aggres-

TABLE 11. PREGNANCY-INDUCED AGGRESSIVE BEHAVIOR IN TWO DIFFERENT GENETIC STOCKS OF MICE[a]

	DBA/2J	C5BL/6J
Proportion (%) agonistic[b]	28/30 (93%)*	17/30 (56%)
Mean (± SEM) composite[c] agonistic score	4.0 (±0.6)	3.6 (± 0.9)
Mean (± SEM) number of tests in which agonistic behavior occurred	2.1 (±0.2)	2.0 (±0.2)

[a]Pregnant mice were assessed for aggressive behavior on Gestation Days 16, 17, and 18 by placing an adult Rockland-Swiss (R-S) male into the homecage of the dam each day for 3 min. The number of attacks and lunges was recorded for each test and a composite aggression score was derived by adding these measures.

[b]On at least one test.

[c]Only for those animals displaying agonistic behavior on at least one test.

*Significantly different, P < .01.

(From Broida and Svare, 1982)

TABLE 12. A COMPARISON OF THE POSTPARTUM AGGRESSIVE BEHAVIOR EXHIBITED BY TWO INBRED MOUSE STRAINS WITH DIFFERENT LEVELS OF REPRODUCTIVE EXPERIENCE

	C57BJ/6J		DBA/2J	
	Primiparous	*Multiparous*	*Primiparous*	*Multiparous*
Proportion (percent) attacking	4/20 (.20)	8/56 (.14)	14/20 (.70)	35/57 (.61)
Median number of attacks[b]	4.0	4.5	4.5	3.7
Proportion (and percent) lunging	0/20 (.00)	3/56 (.05)	10/20 (.50)	21/57 (.37)
Median number of lunges[b]	[c]	1.5	3.7	3.7
Proportion (and percent) lunging or attacking	4/20 (.20)	9/56 (.16)	14/20 (.70)	38/57 (.67)
Median number of lunges and attacks[b]	4.0	4.0	8.2	6.2

Primiparous (one pregnancy) and multiparous (two pregnancies) C57BL/6J and DBA/2J female mice were given a singe three-minute test for aggression between Postpartum Days 4 and 6. An olfactory-bulbectomized adult male Rockland-Swiss albino mouse served as the stimulus animal.

[b]Only for those animals exhibiting the behavior.

[c]Too few animals exhibited the behavior to calculate a median.

(From Broida and Svare, 1982)

sion during pregnancy and lactation and DBA females exhibiting very high levels of the behavior (See Figure 16).

The preliminary work with C57BL/6J and DBA/2J mice clearly ruled out environmental and experiential factors as explanations for the dramatic strain differences we were observing. Furthermore, it laid the groundwork for other experiments designed to look at physiological differences between the two strains and their possible role in gene-related differences in female aggressive behavior. For example, we examined whether or not strain differences in pregnancy-induced aggressive behavior were related to serum progesterone levels. One would expect to see higher levels of progesterone in pregnant DBA/2J mice than C57BL/6J females but we found no such difference (Svare, 1988). (See Figure 17).

When we implanted virgin females of these two strains with silastic capsules containing standard amounts of progesterone, we

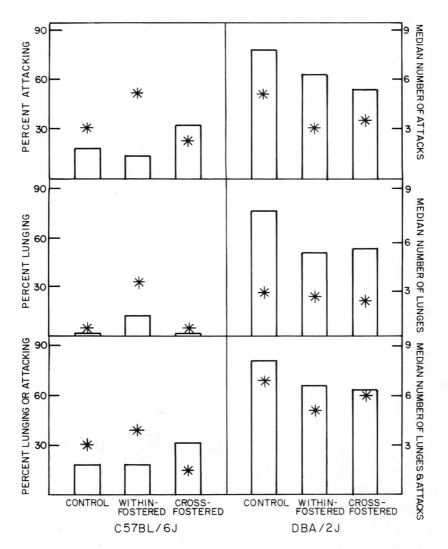

Figure 16. The influence of cross-fostering on strain differences in the maternal aggressive behavior displayed by two inbred mouse strains. The figure shows the percentage of cross-fostered, within-fostered or control C57BL/6J and DBA/2J mice that attacked (top), lunged toward (center), and attacked or lunged toward (bottom) an adult olfactory-bulbectomized Rockland-Swiss albino male mouse. The * represents the median number of attacks, lunges, and attacks and lunges of the aggressive animals in each of the above groups. A single 3-minute test for aggression was conducted between Postpartum Days 4 and 6 (Broida and Svare, 1982).

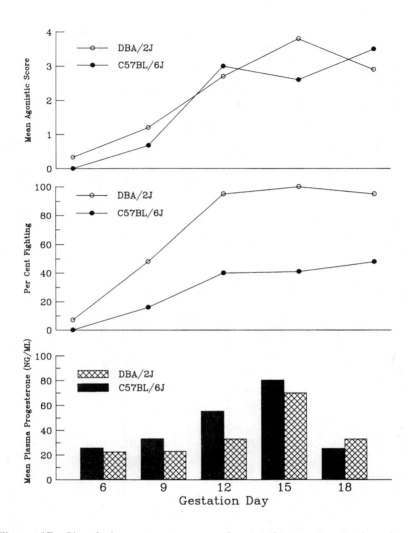

Figure 17. Circulating progesterone values and pregnancy-induced aggressive behavior in C57BL/6J and DBA/2J female mice. The figure shows the mean composite aggression score (top panel), percentage of animals fighting (middle panel), serum progesterone (P) levels (bottom panel) during pregnancy in C57BL/6J and DBA/2J mice. The animals were tested for aggressive behavior on Gestation Days 6, 9, 12, 15, and 18. Separate groups of animals within each strain were blood sampled on Gestation Days 6, 9, 12, 15, or 18 (Svare, 1988).

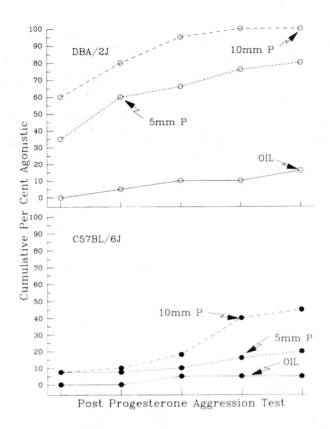

Figure 18. Progesterone stimulation of low aggressive and high aggressive virgin inbred mice. The figure shows the cumulative percentage of adult virgin DBA/2J and C57BL/6J females that exhibited fighting behavior (attacking or lunging) following exposure to a 5-or 10 mm Silastic implant containing progesterone (P) or oil. Following surgery, the animals were tested for aggression every 3 days for a maximum of five tests (15 days of steroid or oil exposure) or were terminated from testing as soon as fighting (either lunging or attacking) occurred (Svare, 1988).

found that the DBA females were much more responsive to the aggression promoting quality of the hormone than were C57BL/6J females (See Figure 18).

Collectively, these studies indicate that genes may be modulating pregnancy-induced aggressive behavior by altering the sensitivity of the brain to progesterone. Genes apparently have shaped the brain of the DBA female to be very sensitive to progesterone while they have shaped the C57BL female's brain to be relatively insensitive to the hormone. Other work in our laboratory is currently exploring whether or not the two strains also differ in terms of serotonergic function. For example, one might expect to see some dynamic of this neurotransmitter to be different in the two strains of mice and this difference might explain in part why DBA/2J females exhibit intense postpartum aggression while C57BL/6J animals do not.

14

Prior Intrauterine Position Can Also Explain Individual Variation in Female Aggressive Behavior

A SECOND FACTOR which seems to play an important role in mediating individual differences in aggressive behavior is a female's intrauterine position that it occupies during fetal life. Mice are classified as polytycous mammals in that they conceive, carry, and deliver multiple offspring in a single litter. Therefore, male and female mice develop in utero (meaning in the uterus or womb) contiguous to (meaning next to) other fetuses of the same and opposite sex (See Figure 19 following page).

Contiguity has dramatic influences on sexually differentiated behavior, physiology, and morphology. For example, female mice that develop in utero between two males (called 2M females) have higher amniotic fluid and fetal blood levels of the male hormone testosterone than females that do not develop next to a male fetus (called 0M females). When compared to 0M females in terms of morphology and behavior, 2M females exhibit longer anogenital spacing at the time of birth. Anogenital spacing is a testosterone dependent event. The more testosterone that is present during

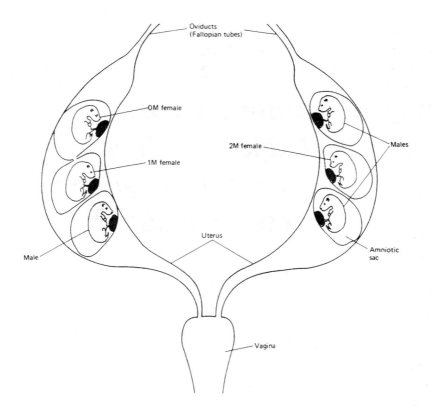

Figure 19. 0M, 1M, and 2M female mouse fetuses in the womb of a pregnant female mouse. (From F.S. vom Saal. In Hormones and Aggressive Behavior, edited by B.B. Svare. New York: Plenum Press, 1983).

fetal life the longer the anogenital spacing. 2M females also exhibit higher levels of certain types of male sexual behavior. Also, research has shown that 2M females are less sexually attractive to males, exhibit longer estrous cycles (called menstrual cycles in human females), achieve puberty later in life, are less proficient in certain types of learning situations, exhibit more locomotor activity, and gain weight more rapidly. Female mice that reside between one male and one female in utero tend to be intermediate in the above reproductive characteristics.

We performed experiments in which we compared female Rockland-Swiss mice derived from different intrauterine locations with respect to pregnancy-induced and postpartum aggression (Kinsley, Miele, Ghiraldi, Konen, and Svare, 1986). The procedure for procuring animals from different intrauterine locations is an interesting one which requires surgical skill and great care. Pregnant mice were humanely sacrificed by cervical dislocation approximately 12 to 16 hours before they normally delivered their offspring naturally.

To perform this surgery, a midline incision is made down the ventrum, the uterine horns are exposed, and each fetus is removed in the order in which they are found. The fetuses are then cleaned with physiological saline, sexed, and their intrauterine location is recorded. The fetuses are then placed on absorbent toweling under heat lamps where they remain for approximately 90 minutes. When the neonates became active they were fostered to other female mice that had just delivered offspring. Just prior to placing the experimental female into the litter, we injected one of its paws with India Ink so that we would be able to distinguish it from the other animals in the litter at the time of weaning. The animals were weaned from the mother at 25 days of age and they were mated with a male at 60 days of age. Some of the animals were then examined for aggressive behavior during pregnancy while other animals were examined for aggressive behavior during lactation.

Our results showed that prior intrauterine position dramatically influenced aggressive behavior exhibited by female mice. 2M female mice (i.e., female mice that had been surrounded by 2 males in the uterus) exhibited many more attacks and lunges during pregnancy as well as during lactation in comparison to 0M females (i.e., female mice that had been surrounded by 2 females in the uterus) (See Figure 20).

We recently performed another experiment in which we sought to explore the importance of the intrauterine environment for female aggressive behavior (Svare and Kinsley, unpublished observations) . In this study, we created female mice that resided alone in the uterus during fetal life and therefore were not exposed to a substantial degree of testosterone during early life. We refer to these animals as "singletons" since they developed in utero without the benefit of stimulation from sibling fetuses. Eight-day pregnant mice

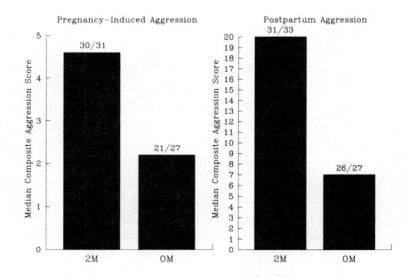

Figure 20. The influence of prior intrauterine location on pregnancy-induced and postpartum aggressive behavior in female mice. Female mice located in utero between two males (2M females) were compared with females residing between no males (0M females) with respect to their aggressive behavior in adulthood on days 15, 16, and 17 of gestation (left panel) and on days 6, 7, and 8 of lactation (right panel). Tests on each day consisted of placing an adult male into the cage of the female for 10 minutes and counting the number of lunges and attacks. These behaviors were summed over the three test days and divided by three to produce a compositie aggression score for each animal during pregnancy and during lactation. The proportions above the histograms represent the proportion of animals fighting on at least one test (Kinsley, Miele, Ghiraldi, Konen, and Svare, 1986).

were surgically prepared so that they carried a single fetus, which was then delivered by cesarean section on Day 18. Control animals consisted of 0M females (females surrounded by 2 females in utero) that were surgically delivered as described in the previous experiment.

When singleton and 0M females were examined for postpartum aggression during adult life, a very interesting pattern of results emerged (See Figure 21). Singleton females seldom displayed

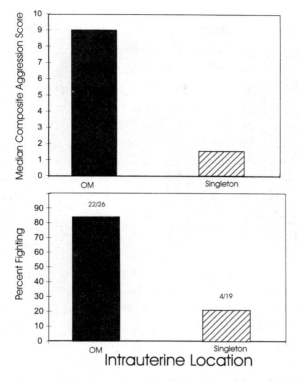

Figure 21. The postpartum aggressive behavior of female mice that developed in utero as singletons or were surrounded by females. The figure shows the postpartum aggressive behavior of singleton female mice, which did not develop with any other fetuses in utero, and females that were surrounded by two females (0M) in utero. The animals were tested for aggressive behavior in adulthood on days 6, 7, and 8 of lactation. Tests on each day consisted of placing an adult male into the cage of the female for 5 minutes and counting the number of lunges and attacks. These behaviors were summed over the three test days and divided by three to produce a composite aggression score for each animal. (The proportion above the histograms represents the proportion of animals fighting on at least one test) (Svare and Kinsley, in preparation).

any aggressive behavior while 0M females exhibited a level of aggression that was low but entirely consistent with that of our previous intrauterine position experiment. Because singleton females do not have the benefit of testosterone exposure from adjacent siblings, it can be concluded that some level of priming with this hormone during fetal life is probably responsible for the development of aggressive behavior in the female.

It is important to note in this experiment that the singleton females were healthy and robust animals, that they exhibited perfectly normal maternal care toward their offspring, and that they exhibited lactation and nursed their young in a manner identical to that of other animals. Though they tended to be larger than 0M females, they could not be distinguished from them in any other aspect of their appearance or behavior. Thus, the absence of aggression in singleton females could not be attributed to any other factor that may have rendered the animals sick, fatigued, or unhealthy.

Our findings with singleton females, if replicated, would appear to have profound implications for our understanding of female aggressive behavior as well as our understanding of just what it means to be a "female." Could it be that true feminine behavior is only achieved through some level of male hormone priming during early life? This is indeed a very exciting question which no doubt could launch many more experiments.

At present, it is not known precisely how an animal's prior intrauterine location and the fetal environment in general modify maternal aggression. However, it is known that fetal testosterone modifies central neural structures (such as the hypothalamus) that probably mediate both pregnancy-induced and postpartum aggression. One could envision a situation then where the hypothalamus is modified by testosterone during early life such that the receipt of aggression promoting biological changes during pregnancy and during lactation are altered. Thus, the receipt of progesterone by the hypothalamus could be fundamentally changed for pregnancy-induced aggression and the receipt of suckling induced changes in serotonin could also be fundamentally altered. This is an intriguing hypothesis which clearly warrants additional research down the road.

15

Influence of the Prenatal Hormone Environment on the Development of Female Aggressive Behaviors

THE INTRAUTERINE LOCATION experiments described in the previous chapter suggested a whole new avenue of research for our group. We reasoned that the development of female aggressive behaviors might depend in part upon how the brain is being shaped and molded by hormonal exposure during early fetal life. For example, it is well known that the brains of mammalian males and females (humans included) are bathed in hormones during early life. Having been exposed to the hormone testosterone from the fetal testes (the endocrine gland that secretes this hormone), males differentiate in a masculine direction. Females on the other hand, which ordinarily are exposed to much lower levels of the male hormone testosterone, differentiate in a feminine direction. Perhaps then some level of hormone exposure is needed for aggressive behavior to appear in the female.

On the basis of the above reasoning, we conducted some simple experiments to explore directly and indirectly whether or not and to what extent the prenatal hormone environment might influence aggressive behavior in females. In one experiment, we used a procedure called prenatal stress to examine indirectly our hypothesis (Kinsley and Svare, 1988). This procedure is known to disrupt the fetal sexual differentiation process and therefore can serve as a technique for exploring prenatal hormone contributions to maternal aggression.

In the prenatal stress procedure, pregnant female mice were placed into Plexiglas restraint tubes for a period of 30 minutes, 3 times a day on the 13th through 19th days of gestation. While in the restraint tubes, the animals were also exposed to flood lamps that were placed above them. When the animals delivered, their female offspring were given (fostered) to another mother (unstressed) that had just recently delivered. This was done in order to prevent any possible differences due to the postnatal rearing environment and is a standard procedure in this kind of experimentation. When the females became adult, they were mated and examined for their aggressive behavior during pregnancy and during lactation. The results of the experiment showed that the prenatal stress procedure dramatically reduced aggressive behavior during pregnancy and significantly elevated the behavior during the postpartum state (See Figure 22).

Interpreting these prenatal stress results was not easy but we felt strongly that something was happening to the manner in which the stressed animals were being exposed to hormones during early life. For example, some research by other psychologists had already shown that prenatal stress disturbs the timing of testosterone secretion during fetal life and in some cases actually lowers the amount of the hormone that is secreted.

To further explore the possibility that prenatal stress was influencing testosterone secretion, we examined the anogenital length of the females when they were born. As noted earlier, this biological marker is indicative of how much testosterone animals have been exposed to during prenatal life. Males typically have much longer anogenital distances than do females since the former are exposed to higher levels of testosterone prenatally. Our results showed that anogenital distances in prenatally stressed females were actually shorter (See Table 13), suggesting that they had been exposed to less testosterone during early critical periods of sexual differentiation.

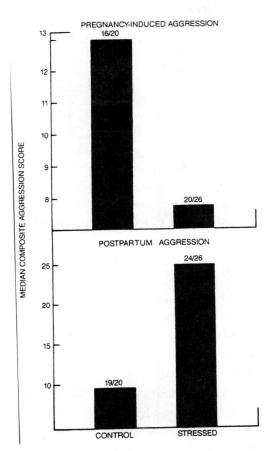

Figure 22. The influence of prenatal stress on the pregnancy-induced and postpartum aggressive behavior of female mice. The figure shows the median composite aggression score (lunges and attacks) exhibited by prenatally-stressed (STRESSED) and control (CONTROL) Rockland-Swiss (R-S) albino mice during pregnancy (top panel) and lactation (bottom panel). Numbers above the histograms refer to the proportion of animals exhibiting fighting (either lunging or attacking) on at least one test during pregnancy or lactation. Medians were computed only for those animals exhibiting aggression on at least one test. Heat and restraint stress was administered three times a day between days 13 and 18 of gestation. Following mating at 60-80 days of age, the animals were tested for pregnancy-induced aggressive behavior on three consecutive days (Gestation Days 15, 16, and 17). For aggression testing, an unfamiliar adult R-S male (70–90 days of age) was placed into the female's cage for 10 minutes (Kinsley and Svare, 1988).

TABLE 13. THE ANOGENITAL LENGTH OF FEMALE MICE THAT WERE STRESSED DURING FETAL LIFE

Group	N	AGD	BW	Relative AGD
Prenatally-Stressed	47	0.62 (±0.01)*	1.30 (±0.02)*	47.7 (±1.02)**
Control	34	0.81 (±0.01)	1.44 (±0.03)	55.9 (±1.24)

Mean (±S.E.M.) (+) anogenital distance (AGD) (mm), body weight (BW) (g), and relative AGD (AGD/BW x 100) at birth for prenatally-stressed and control Rockland-Swiss (R-S) female mice.
*Significantly different from controls, p < 0.0001.
**Significantly different from controls, p < 0.01
(From Kinsley and Svare, 1988)

Our data showing that prenatally stressed females exhibited lower levels of aggression during pregnancy fit this scenario quite nicely but the data showing elevated postpartum aggression in prenatally stressed females ran contrary to this hypothesis. At this point, we strongly felt that we needed to conduct more experimentation in order to more fully investigate the dynamics of the prenatal hormone environment and what its role might be in the development of female aggressive behavior.

Another way to explore the role of the prenatal hormone environment is to inject pregnant female mice with very low doses of virilizing hormones, like testosterone, and then examine what happens to the aggressive behavior of the offspring once they grow up and are mated as adults. We performed an experiment in which pregnant females were injected with very low doses of testosterone (.5, 1, or 2 µg of testosterone) on the 12th, 14th, and 16th days of gestation (Mann and Svare, 1983). This period of fetal life is a time during which sexual differentiation is taking place and the brain is very sensitive to hormones. The female offspring were allowed to grow up and were tested for aggressive behavior once they were mated with male mice.

Our results showed that the prenatal injections of testosterone (at least at the two higher doses) elevated aggressive behavior but they seemed to do so in the absence of any effects upon external morphology. That is, the anogenital distance of the prenatally testosterone exposed females was indistinguishable from that of control females (See Table 14).

Another hormone that reaches very high levels in the plasma of

TABLE 14. THE POSTPARTUM AGGRESSIVE BEHAVIOR OF FEMALE MICE THAT WERE TREATED DURING FETAL LIFE WITH SMALL AMOUNTS OF TESTOSTERONE

Group	Proportion (and %) Attacking on at Least One Test	Median (and range) Latency (in days) to Exhibit Attacking*	Median (and range) Number of Attacks*	Median (and range) Number of Test Days Fighting*
NIC	43/48 (90)	1.0 (1.0–2.0)	6.7 (1.3–13.3)	3.0 (2.0–3.0)
OIL	44/48 (92)	1.0 (1.0–2.0)	6.5 (0.7–15.3)	3.0 (2.0–3.0)
0.5 μg TP	53/53 (100)	1.0 (1.0–2.0)	7.7 (2.3–18.3)	3.0 (2.0–3.0)
1.0 μg TP	50/50 (100)	1.0 (1.0–3.0)	9.4 (0.3–20.0)**	3.0 (1.0–3.0)
2.0 μg TP	43/56 (94)	1.0 (1.0–2.0)	8.3 (1.0–20.3)**	3.0 (2.0–3.0)

*Of those animals exhibiting attacking.
**Significantly different from Groups NIC and OIL, $p < 0.05$.
Separate groups of timed-mated pregnant Rockland-Swiss (R-S) females were given a single injection of 0.5, 1.0, or 2.0 μg of testosterone propionate (TP) in 0.05 cc sesame oil or the oil vehicle alone on Gestation Days 12, 14, and 16 for a total of 3 injections. A separate group of animals was not injected. Upon delivery, all litters were culled to 6–8 female pups and were then fostered to untreated dams. At 60 days of age, the females were mated with adult R-S males and isolated when a copulatory plug was found. Three-minute tests for aggression against an adult R-S male were conducted on Postpartum Days 6, 7, and 8 for a total of 3 tests.
(From Mann and Svare, 1983)

developing fetal females is the hormone progesterone. Indeed, some scientists have proposed that progesterone actually serves to protect the female brain during fetal life by preventing testosterone from entering brain cells in the hypothalamus. Alternatively, another group of scientists feels that the hormone actually can do the opposite. That is, if sufficient quantities of progesterone are in circulation, they can actually act like the masculinizing hormone testosterone! Indeed, progesterone and testosterone are very similar to each other in terms of their biochemistry and research in humans and animals supports the contention that masculinization, in part or whole, can occur with exposure to this steroid.

We performed an experiment with prenatal progesterone exposure that was very similar to the one reviewed above in which we used prenatal testosterone treatments. Pregnant female mice were injected with 250 or 500 μg of progesterone a day from the 12th to the 16th day of pregnancy. When the animals delivered their off-spring, the females were fostered to mothers who had just recently delivered and had not been exposed to hormone injections. As is standard for this kind of experimentation, we also included groups of pregnant females that were injected with sesame oil (the placebo) or were not injected at all (non-injected control). We allowed these females to grow up into adulthood and then we mated them in a manner identical to that of the other experiments. After they delivered offspring, we then examined their aggressive behavior during the postpartum period on the 6th, 7th, and 8th days of lactation. Interestingly, we found that both dosages of progesterone elevated postpartum aggression and they also increased anogenital spacing. These findings therefore suggested that progesterone was acting by partially masculinizing the brain (See Table 15 and Figure 23).

Our research examining prenatal manipulations (stress and hormone treatments) and their effects on female aggression resulted in tremendous individual variation. You probably noticed from the tables and figures that some animals would respond to these treatments with substantial changes in aggressive behavior

TABLE 15. THE EFFECTS OF PRENATAL PROGESTERONE EXPOSURE ON ANOGENITAL DISTANCE IN FEMALE MICE

Group	N	Body Weight (g)	Anogenital Distance (mm)	Relative Anogenital Distance[a]
NIC	29	1.51 ± 0.03[b]	0.84 ± 0.01	55.62 ± 0.97[b]
Oil	33	1.51 ± 0.02	0.85 ± 0.01	56.29 ± 0.88
250 µg P	29	1.47 ± 0.03	0.98 ± 0.02	60.54 ± 1.32*
500 µg P	36	1.48 ± 0.03	0.86 ± 0.01	58.12 ± 1.06**

The body weights, anogenital distances, and relative anogenital distances of female Rockland-Swiss albino mice that were prenatally treated with progesterone or oil or were noninjected. The animals were injected daily on days 12 through 16 of gestation. The assessments were made on the day of birth. P = progesterone; NIC = noninjected.

[a]Anogenital distance/body weight x 100.

[b]Mean ± SEM.

*Significantly different from Groups NIC and OIL ($P < 0.05$).

**Significantly different from Group NIC ($P < 0.05$).

(From Konen, Kinsley, and Svare, 1986)

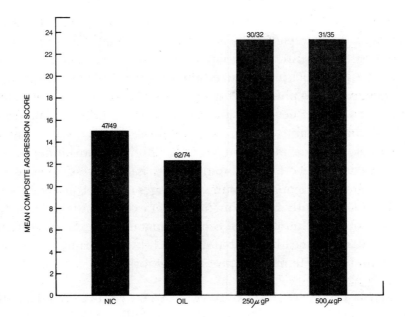

Figure 23. The influence of prenatal progesterone exposure on the post-partum aggressive behavior of female mice. The figure shows the mean composite aggression score (number of attacks and lunges) for female Rockland-Swiss (R-S) albino mice that were treated prenatally with progesterone (P) (250 µg or 500 µg) or oil (OIL) or were noninjected (NIC). Pregnant animals were injected daily on Days 12 through 16 of gestation. Upon delivery, all litters were culled to 5–7 female pups and were then fostered to untreated dams. At 60 days of age, the females were mated with adult R-S males and isolated when a copulatory plug was found. Five-minute tests for postpartum aggression against an adult R-S male mouse were conducted on Postpartum Days, 6, 7, and 8. (Konen, Kinsley, and Svare, 1986).

while other animals showed no changes. Because genotype could be mediating this individual variation, we conducted another experiment in which we examined prenatal stress effects on the aggressive behavior of inbred C57BL/6J and DBA/2J mice (Kinsley and Svare, 1987). The experiment was conducted in a manner identical to that of the experiment in which we explored the effects of prenatal stress on female aggressive behavior in our outbred mice (Rockland-Swiss).

Our results showed that prenatal stress exerted its effects on postpartum aggression in a strain dependent manner. That is, prenatal stress significantly increased postpartum aggression in C57BL/6J females and reduced the behavior in DBA/2J females. It is important to note that the results we obtained occurred in the absence of any effects upon anogenital spacing in the females (See Figure 24 and Table 16).

These findings clearly suggest that prenatal hormone conditions play a role in the development of female aggressive behavior. However, the exact nature of those changes remains obscure at this point. We currently are conducting other experiments in which we are examining the effects of other prenatal hormone treatments (as well as drug treatments that selectively block hormones) on the development of female aggressive behaviors.

TABLE 16. THE ANOGENITAL DISTANCES OF FEMALE INBRED MICE THAT WERE STRESSED DURING PRENATAL LIFE.

Group	N	AGD	BW	Relative AGD
C57BL/6J males				
Control	35	1.28 (± .02)	1.29 (± .02)	99.2 (+ 1.79)
Prenatally stressed	23	1.13 (± .02)***	1.08 (± .02)***	106.4 (+ 2.32)**
C57BK/6J females				
Control	27	.67 (± .02)	1.27 (± .02)	52.9 (+1.50)
Prenatally stressed	27	.58 (± .01)**	1.09 (± .02)***	52.7 (+ 1.65)
DBA/2J males				
Control	18	1.43 (± .04)	1.26 (± .03)	113.5 (+ 4.26)
Prenatally stressed	34	1.15 (± .02)**	1.25 (± .03)	91.9 (+ 2.82)**
DBA/2J females				
Control	14	.79 (± .04)	1.25 (± .04)	62.9 (+ 3.38)
Prenatally stressed	16	.69 (± .03)*	1.13 (± .04)*	61.2 (+ 2.98)

Mean (± SEM) anogenital distance (AGD) (mm), body weight (BW) (g), and relative AGD (AGD/BW x 100) at birth for prenatally stressed and control C57BL/6J and DBA/2J male and female mice.

* Significantly different from same strain, same sex control, $p <$ .02.

** Significantly different from same strain, same sex control, $p <$ .01.

*** Significantly different from same strain, same sex control, $p <$ .001.

(From Kinsley and Svare, 1987)

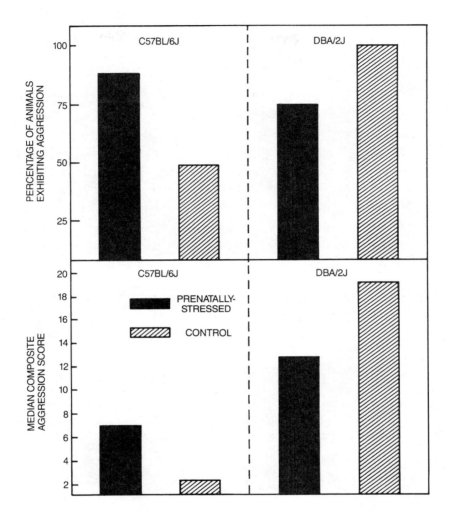

Figure 24. The influence of prenatal stress on the postpartum aggressive behavior of two different inbred strains of mice. The figure shows the percentage of animals exhibiting postpartum aggression (on at least one test day) (a) and the median composite aggression score (of those animals exhibiting lunging or attacking on at least 1 test day) (b) for prenatally stressed and control C57BL/6J and DBA/2J female mice. Heat and restraint stress was administered three times a day between Days 13 and 18 of gestation. Following mating at 60 days of age, the animals were tested for postpartum aggression on 3 consecutive days (Postpartum Days 4, 5, and 6). For aggression testing, an unfamiliar weight-matched Rockland-Swiss (R-S) male mouse was placed into the female's cage for 10 minutes (Kinsley and Svare, 1987)

Part V

PROXIMATE AND ULTIMATE CAUSATION

16

How Do Physiological Changes Mediate Alterations in Female Aggressive Behavior?

To BRIEFLY REVIEW some of our work at this point, we documented that progesterone promotes aggression during pregnancy, estrogen suppresses it shortly following parturition, and suckling induced alterations in serotonergic (and perhaps opioid) function facilitate fighting behavior during lactation.

Just how the above physiological alterations mediate changes in aggressive behavior is not understood. However, the transition from passivity (virgin state), to threat behavior (pregnancy), to docility (postpartum estrous), to intense aggression (early lactation), back to passivity (late lactation) may be related to fundamental changes in perceptual processes and resulting changes in the motivational impact of sensory stimuli.

Mice are olfactory guided animals. It would seem logical therefore that changes in aggressive behavior during pregnancy and lactation could reflect changes in the female's sensitivity to olfactory cues from conspecifics. Thus, another avenue of our research program has been to examine the reaction of female mice to urinary cues from other male and female mice (Miele and Svare, unpublished).

Female mice were placed into a standard mouse cage that was lined with filter paper (See Figure 25). The cage contained 6 drops

103

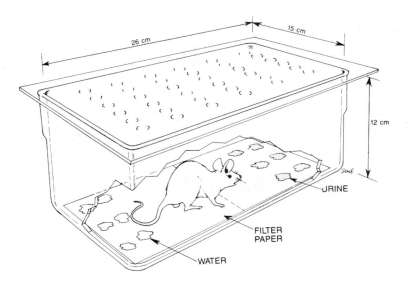

Figure 25. A female mouse in an olfactory preference chamber. The cage (ll X 7 X 5 inches) consists of filter paper on the floor and a perforated Plexiglas top. Urine is placed on one side of the filter paper and water is placed on the other side. The control condition consists of water placed on both sides. Subjects were placed in the middle of the chamber and the amount of time spent on each side was recorded in a 5 minute test session. Animals were recorded as exhibiting a preference when all 4 paws were on one side of the apparatus. The animal in the diagram is exhibiting a preference for the water side of the chamber (Svare, 1989, Miele and Svare, unpublished observations).

of adult male urine on one side and 6 drops of tap water on the other side. A control condition consisted of the same filter paper lined cage with 6 drops of tap water on each side of the cage. Separate groups of pregnant females were tested for their preferences in the cage (5-minute test) on either Gestation Day 6, or 18 or Postpartum Day 8, 14, or 20.

Early in gestation (Day 6) and late in lactation (Day 20) females showed no preference and spent roughly equal amounts of time on the water and male urine sides. In contrast, females that were tested late in gestation (Day 18) or in early to midlactation (Day 8 or 14) tended to avoid male urine and spent far less time on the urine side in contrast to the water side (See Figure 26).

These findings would seem to be important for two reasons. First they show that female mice find male urine to be aversive and will avoid a substrate that is coated with this olfactory cue. Second, they show that the stage of the reproductive cycle is important in determining the aversiveness of male urine. Male urine appears to be most aversive to late gestation females and mid-lactating animals. Most importantly, however, differences in olfactory preferences are associated with differences in aggressive behavior over the reproductive cycle. Male urine is apparently most aversive when aggression is the highest (late gestation and early to mid-lactation) and least aversive when aggression is lowest (early gestation and late lactation).

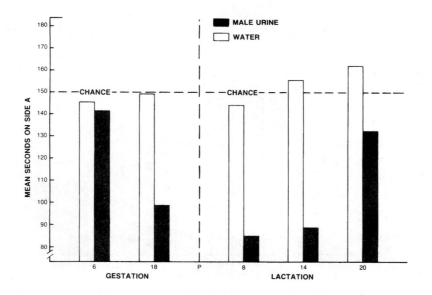

Figure 26. The olfactory preferences of pregnant and lactating female mice. The figure shows the amount of time that pregnant and lactating female mice investigated filter paper that was exposed to water on one side and male urine on the other side. A control condition consisted of animals exposed to filter paper that was exposed to water on both sides. Tests were 5 minutes in duration (Svare, 1989; Miele and Svare, unpublished observations).

We performed an additional experiment to examine the influence of different types of urine on olfactory preferences in female mice (Miele and Svare, unpublished observations). Early lactating females (Postpartum Day 8) were tested for their reaction to substrates that were soiled with lactating female urine, virgin female urine, or male urine. Once again, the control condition consisted of filter paper containing tap water on each side.

Lactating female mice found the substrate containing male urine to be the most aversive; the least aversive urine was that of other lactating female mice while urine from virgin female mice was intermediate in producing avoidance (See Figure 27). These

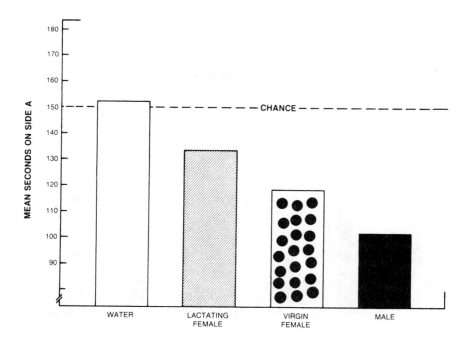

Figure 27. The olfactory preferences of lactating female mice toward different types of urine. The figure shows the amount of time lactating female mice spent investigating urine or water contaminated filter paper during a 5 minute test session. Urine from males, lactating females or virgin females was used as stimuli. A control condition consisted of filter paper with tap water on each side (Svare, 1989; Miele and Svare, unpublished observations).

findings provide an interesting parallel to what is known concerning the elicitation of postpartum aggressive behavior by intruder animals. Some of our earlier research had shown that lactating female mice attack males most intensely and other lactating females least intensely while virgin females tend to elicit intermediate levels of attack (Svare and Gandelman, 1973; Svare, Betteridge, Katz, and Samuels, 1981).

The findings reviewed in this part of our research program may help us to understand just how aggression altering neuroendocrine changes exert their effects on the pregnant and lactating mouse. Mice, like other rodents, are olfactory guided animals, and the neuroendocrine changes that alter aggression during gestation and the postpartum period may produce their effects by changing the motivational impact of olfactory cues from conspecifics. Stimuli that ordinarily are neutral or only mildly aversive may become highly aversive or even preferred as the reproductive condition of the female changes. Therefore, neuroendocrine changes responsible for aggressive behavior in the female may produce their effects by altering fundamental perceptual/sensory processes.

17

Summarizing What We Know About the Proximate Causes of Female Aggressive Behavior

OUR RESEARCH HAS identified some of the more important proximate biological and behavioral causes of aggression in the female mouse. To briefly review, virgin female mice exhibit little if any aggressive behavior toward other adults. However, once a female becomes pregnant, her behavior toward other animals, especially males, dramatically changes. Aggression increases during pregnancy, declines shortly following the delivery of young, is very high several days into lactation (nursing of young), and declines as the offspring advance in age. Progesterone stimulates aggression during pregnancy and estrogen suppresses it in the hours following parturition. Intense aggression begins to develop after the postpartum female has received about 48 hours of suckling stimulation from her young.

It is well documented that the onset of postpartum aggression following the delivery of young is contingent upon two elements. First, estrogen and progesterone induce growth of the overall size and length of the teats during pregnancy. The growth of the teats, referred to as the substrate preparation phase, is an important process during pregnancy since newborns otherwise would not be able to attach and suckle from the mother if it did not occur. Second the receipt of suckling stimulation from young is essential for the establishment of fighting behavior during the postpartum period. Aggressive behavior does not develop if either one of these elements (growth of the nipples or suckling stimulation from young) is missing.

Therefore, steroid hormone exposure during pregnancy stimulates female aggressive behavior in two ways: First, it directly promotes threat behavior during pregnancy; Second, it indirectly stimulates aggression during the postpartum period by preparing the substrate (growth of the nipples) for attachment and suckling stimulation from young.

The receipt of suckling stimulation during the nursing process is a critical factor in the establishment of aggressive behavior during the postpartum period. Not only does this event turn on the synthesis and release of milk (called lactation), but it also promotes defensive behavior on the part of the female. Suckling-induced changes in serotonergic (and perhaps opioid) function modulate the onset of aggressive behavior during the postpartum period.

Fundamental changes in perceptual processes that are mediated by the above neuroendocrine changes, may be responsible for behavioral changes in aggressiveness that fluctuate with the reproductive cycle. In particular, the motivational impact of olfactory cues from intruders may be altered by neuroendocrine status and, therefore, contribute to changes in aggression.

Although suckling stimulation is critical for the establishment of aggressive behavior in the postpartum mouse, it apparently is not needed on a continuous basis. As shown by our research, if pups are removed for one hour during early lactation, postpartum aggression is not affected. However, 5 hours of pup removal all but eliminates aggressive behavior in the postpartum female. Interestingly, if young are replaced for as little as 5 minutes following 5 hours of pup removal, the behavior is restored almost immediately.

Direct physical contact between the mother and her young is not a prerequisite for the short-term maintenance of the behavior. Placement of the mother's litter behind a double wire mesh partition in the home cage maintains the behavior at a level indistinguishable from mothers in direct contact with their young.

Finally, aggression declines as the pups get older and this corresponds to the changing dynamics of the mother young interaction; postpartum female mice typically nurse their young for shorter bouts of time as their offspring get older and eventually are able to feed on their own. One must presume that suckling-induced changes in the hypothalamus are also responsible for the decline in aggression as pups get older as well as the exteroceptive maintenance of the behavior by young.

Our work also shows that individual variation in maternal aggression is related in part to genotype and to prior in utero position. C57BL/J6 female mice exhibit very low levels of female aggressive behavior while DBA/2J mice exhibit very high levels of aggression. Our research shows that these strain differences may be mediated by genotype-based differences in progesterone sensitivity as well as differences in suckling induced serotonergic function in the brain.

Our research also shows that females that were surrounded by two males (called 2M females) during intrauterine life exhibited higher levels of pregnancy-induced and postpartum aggression than females that were surrounded by 2 females during intrauterine life (called 0M females). Interestingly, female mice that are not exposed to any siblings in utero (singleton females) fail to develop aggressive behavior. Thus, the prenatal hormone environment and intrauterine location may influence aggression by altering testosterone-dependent brain areas during early critical periods of sexual differentiation.

Finally, in addition to the intrauterine position experiments, other findings from our laboratory also implicate the prenatal hormone environment in the development of female aggressive behavior. Prenatal stress, a procedure that alters fetal steroid hormone levels, reduces pregnancy-induced aggressive behavior and elevates postpartum aggression. Genetic background alters responsiveness to stress. Prenatally stressed C57BL/6J mice exhibit elevations in postpartum aggressive behavior while prenatally stressed DBA/2J mice exhibit a reduction in the behavior. Also, prenatal injections of testosterone or progesterone, hormones that are known to virilize the mammalian brain during early periods of sexual differentiation, elevate levels of postpartum aggression in RS female mice.

18

Considering Questions of Ultimate Causation: Female Aggression Viewed as an Optimization Problem

MUCH OF OUR RESEARCH has focused on questions of the immediate biological and physiological factors governing aggressive behavior in pregnant and lactating female mice. Questions of ultimate causation (ie., What is the functional significance of this behavior?) are equally important but much less studied by our research group. These are questions which will help to stimulate our future research in this area as well as the investigations of others. Let us consider some of these issues since it will help to put into focus how this behavior fits into the total social and evolutionary history of the mouse.

It is quite obvious that aggression exhibited by pregnant and lactating female mice probably serves to protect offpsring from other animals that might harm them when they are young and defenseless. The adaptive function of this seems readily apparent—survival of the species! However, and perhaps more importantly, the mother's ability to pass on her own genes in her offspring is contingent upon how well she is able to protect and defend her young.

The behavior that we call maternal aggression or maternal defense may have evolved as a counterstrategy for a behavior often exhibited by many male mammals and this is called infanticide, or the killing of young. If a male happens upon a female nursing newborns and the newborns are not his, the male is likely to try and kill the pups so that he can then mate with the mother to produce his own young and continue his genes. Thus, maternal defense probably co-evolved with infanticide and there is a considerable body of literature that now exists to confirm this hypothesis.

Maternal protective behavior can be defined from a number of different perspectives (Svare and Boechler, 1994). It can be characterized by exploring outcomes (ie., do pups survive or are they killed?), it can be defined in terms of the receiver of such behaviors (ie., are intruders attacked or are they left alone?), and it can be explored by studying the maternal female (ie., is the female victorious or defeated?).

In situations where we have explored the proximate mechanisms modulating the behavior in mice, we have defined maternal protective behavior in very pragmatic terms. That is, the female is declared to be maternally aggressive if she exhibits attacks or lunges toward a strange intruder male mouse introduced to her cage. Test periods typically are short (only several minutes in duration) and there is no attempt to examine any of the other outcomes listed above. When examining ultimate mechanisms however, questions of behavioral outcomes become more important and it is necessary to broaden our definition of what we call maternal protective behavior. In these situations (questions of ultimate causation), one could consider maternal protective behaviors to be aggressive behaviors exhibited by the female that decrease the probability that an intruder will harm young, while simultaneously increasing the likelihood of injury or death to the mother.

In view of the different scope of questions asked by those interested in proximate causality versus those interested in ultimate causality, it is not surprising that different types of methodologies have emerged. For example, in our laboratory we have utilized a relatively simple procedure for studying the proximate behavioral and biological mechanisms underlying female aggressive behavior exhibited by Rockland-Swiss albino mice. As previously stated, our animals are generated as an outbred stock and females are used in experiments beginning at 60 days of age. At this time, they are housed with stud males and are isolated when a copulatory plug is found. At parturition (19 days following impregnation) litters typically are adjusted to 6 pups and the young are weaned at 21 days of age.

For the purposes of aggression tests, sexually naive males are placed into the cage of the female for 3 minutes and attacks and lunges exhibited by the female are scored. In cases where females are being tested in the postpartum state, pups are removed shortly before the test to avoid their potentially confounding role in the behavior exhibited by the resident female. Adult male intruders that have been group housed (6/cage) are used as opponents since they elicit high levels of attack and usually do not fight back in response to being attacked.

The methods employed for assessing questions of ultimate causation utilize far different procedures including semi-natural environments with nest boxes and entrances and exits that can be manipulated in such a way to allow or prevent access by intruders. Other tactics also include the imposition of environmental constraints upon the female, such as foraging requirements. The simultaneous assessment of maternal protective behavior and infanticide in these situations is a powerful tool for exploring questions of ultimate causation.

It is very important to note that no single method for assessing maternal protective behavior is necessarily better than any other. Each has its advantages and its limitations. For example, utilizing sexually naive intruder males of unknown rank provides a standard stimulus for aggression tests when examining questions of proximate causation. However, intruder dominance/subordinance status and previous sexual experience may alter the exhibition of maternal aggression and therefore may represent an important variable for consideration. Likewise, isolating females in studies designed to examine proximate questions may duplicate what happens in wild female mice that are known to live in a solitary fashion, but they obviously do not replicate the communal rearing situation that is often seen in other mouse social organizations. The point here is that something is lost and something is gained with each strategy that is employed. Oversimplification of the test situation limits our generalizability to the wild while duplication of semi-natural environments limits our ability to control single variables and determine cause and effect relationships. Regardless, we must be content as scientists to confine our conclusions to the strategies employed in our testing situations.

A different avenue of research possibilities has emerged in our laboratory as we have started to view maternal aggression as an optimization problem. In other words, we have started to look at this behavior in the context of ultimate causation. Let us examine some of these unique and interesting questions.

The intensity of nest defense performed by a parent entails some risk (injury or death) and results in some benefits (increased probablility of offspring survival). Therefore, a cost-benefit analysis can be used to predict optimum level of defense in a given situation. Consider for example the development and decline of aggression over pregnancy and lactation. Changes in aggressive behavior can be compared to what is known about parental defense theory. For example, maternal protective behavior during pregnancy increases as the reproductive value of the young increases, but is still quite low in comparison to what happens during lactation. Thus, the female should take relatively low risks and, as noted earlier, only threat behavior (lunges) is exhibited at this time. Risk taking (e.g., aggression) increases after parturition as the reproductive value of the young increases. Thus, increasing benefits to the female are being derived and elevated aggression (and its increasing costs) is evident. However, once the young begin to leave the nest, their value to the female continues to increase. Likewise, benefits from defense decline because juveniles are more capable of escaping danger and adult male intruders probably are not capable of destroying an entire litter once it has started dispersing from the nest.

Two stages of the reproductive cycle of the female would initially appear to contradict the optimization analysis advanced here. First, in the early postpartum period (postpartum estrous), the female does not protect her young even against a strange male intruder. It must be assumed that enormous benefits can be derived from mating again and becoming pregnant since the female would be able to produce many more young and her fitness would be greatly enhanced. If one assumes that the new male is a dominant male and is therefore more "fit" (e.g., better genes), it could be advantageous for the female to abandon (i.e., not protect) her current offspring and mate again. The benefits of this behavior may outweigh the costs to the female if the offspring produced by the second mating are more "fit" than the young produced by the first mating.

Second, it would initially appear to be paradoxical that maternal protective behavior declines before young disperse. It is well know that females suckle their young less during this period and that they actively reject them at the nipple. The benefit here also involves the production of new offspring. The female will begin to ovulate sooner if she is suckled less. Thus, she can mate again, produce more young in a shorter period of time, and elevate her lifetime fitness. The benefit of initiating reproduction sooner may outweigh the cost/risk of continued defense.

Some studies in our laboratory have attempted to explore some of the many questions concerning ultimate causation and maternal protective behavior. Several of these experiments are briefly reviewed here so that you can get a feel for the direction of a whole different avenue of research that is spinning off from our original work.

As reviewed earlier, removal of young during lactation terminates maternal defense (Svare and Gandelman, 1973; Svare, 1977). Also, you will recall that pregnancy termination dramatically lowers aggressive behavior (Svare, Miele, and Kinsley, 1986). From parental defense theory, it of course makes no sense to continue to engage in defense when the reproductive value of your offspring is zero. When compared to the high aggressive behavior of sham-operated pregnant females, pregnancy terminated females failed to engage in any aggressive behavior when challenged with an adult male intruder.

A second recent experiment dealing with parental investment theory concerns what happens to females of different fighting ability and the allocations they make to the two sexes (Svare and Boechler, unpublished observations). Under ideal conditions, parental investment theory predicts that sons should be favored over daughters since the former can produce more offspring. In two different experiments, we assessed aggressive behavior during pregnancy and fetal sex ratio. Our findings showed that highly aggressive females produced more males than medium or low aggressive females.

The mentioning of one final experiment that was completed recently in our laboratory has a strong bearing on some of the work that we hope is continued in this area. This work concerns the relationship between maternal protective behavior and the spontaneous killing of young typically exhibited by females with very large litters. Postpartum female mice often kill their own young even when environmental conditions are favorable (ie., food is freely available).

With data collected on over 100 lactating female RS mice, we found the following: (1) Roughly 35–40% off R-S mice exhibit killing of young; (2) The larger the litter size, the greater the liklihood that females will display infanticide; (3) The killing of young usually occurs early in lactation; (4) Those animals that kill young and those that do not are identical with respect to aggressive behavior, lactation performance, and the ability to rear young. Therefore, the killing of young by the postpartum female is not an aberrant behavior but rather it represents an adaptive strategy that does not compromise the maternal caretaking or defensive behavior of the mother.

19

Putting It All Together: Why is the Study of Female Aggressive Behavior Important?

"I may be a dreamer, an incurable optimist, but I believe that if science provides knowledge, a society will display wisdom."

Frank Beach (From: The perpetuation and evolution of biological science. *American Psychologist,* 1979, 21, 943–949)

PRACTITIONERS OF BASIC science pursue research questions because they find the phenomena they are studying to be intrinsically interesting in their own right. That is to say, they often care very little whether or not and to what extent their research topic will help mankind in some practical way. As a basic scientist I can honestly say that this has always been the case with my own particular research pursuits. However, I believe that the study of female aggressive behavior does have some practical benefit beyond that of just understanding how and why this behavior works in the way in which it does.

First, at one time it was thought that the ability to display aggressive behavior was strictly the domain of the male. It was thought that the female, the so-called "weaker" sex, simply lacked the underlying neural architecture that would allow it to display a behavior that was thought only to exist in the male. Clearly, our findings show that the female is quite capable of displaying very intense aggression that is equal to if not greater than that exhibited by the male. The myths regarding the "docile" and "passive" female therefore have been shattered by our findings. No one can ever claim again that females do not have the strength, the underlying neural substrate, or the motivation to exhibit aggression.

Second, exploring changes in behavior as they occur over pregnancy and lactation in the mouse may help us to better understand mood changes that are known to occur in human females going through similar reproductive states. In human females, pregnancy, parturition, and lactation are accompanied by emotional changes and in certain cases psychiatric illness. For example, it is not uncommon to see heightened levels of depression, irritability, mood swings, neuroses, as well as violence and hostility during the peripartum period in human females. Perhaps these behavioral changes in humans represent the vestiges of maternal aggressive behavior observed in lower mammals.

Normal changes as well as those considered to be aberrant such as postpartum psychosis and the postpartum blues syndrome are thought to have an underlying physiological basis. Although speculation has centered around the role of hormone and neurotransmitter changes, little research has been conducted in humans to explore these possibilities. In the future, our research with mice may provide helpful information and departure points for researchers exploring behavioral changes in pregnant and lactating humans.

Finally, preclinical screening of new drugs for their effectiveness in the treatment of a wide array of human behavior disorders requires the use of animal models. In particular, the quest for the development of new and better antipsychotic and antidepressant drugs now routinely includes an evaluation of their effects on the maternal aggressive behavior exhibited by female mice. Prior to our elucidation of the mechanisms controlling aggression in the female, drug screening for changes in mood usually consisted of assessing behavioral responses in male rodents alone. Information derived from these studies therefore was gender biased and may not have generalized to that of the female. Examining drug effects upon female aggressive behavior will allow the psychopharmacologist to provide a more complete profile of a drug's potential efficacy in the treatment of mental disorder.

20

Some Final Thoughts

THE RESEARCH PRESENTED here represents the highlights of over 25 years of laboratory-based basic research. Through it all, interesting hypotheses have been proven, chance observations have produced provocative results, and numerous failures have caused a rethinking of the research road and where to go next. This is all part of any scientific endeavor and it is certainly not unique to psychological inquiry. Hopefully, you as new students of psychology, now have a much better picture of how a psychologist goes about his work.

The thousands of hours we have spent in experimentation, observation, analysis, thought and discussion have contributed to the understanding of a behavior that is exhibited by almost all mammalian species. Defense of young plays an important role in species survival and social organization. Therefore, continued research on the biological and behavioral underpinnings of female aggression would seem to be a worthy research topic for the future.

Researchers from many different disciplines are now exploring aggressive behavior exhibited by pregnant and lactating females. Both field research as well as laboratory based studies are being conducted with other rodents (rats, hamsters, guinea pigs), as well as sheep, cows, cats, langurs, and gelada baboons. Investigations on other species conducted by other researchers are critical to establishing both the validity and reliability of our findings with mice. We look forward with great anticipation to those findings as well as the results from continuing research studies in our own laboratory. Clearly, the totality of all this information will ultimately be needed to fully establish the laws that govern this behavior.

I have stated to my students many times that the acquisition of knowledge through scientific inquiry is like building a huge pyramid. It takes an extraordinary amount of time to lay the foundation and then proceed step by step with its construction. Each new block builds upon another existing piece. All parts are interrelated and must be cemented with each other in order to advance along to the top...the finished product. The complexity of studying behavior requires that one proceed slowly and methodically. With each answer that emerges, many more new and interesting questions evolve. Therefore, as you can see here, a psychologist's quest never really ends and complete closure on a research topic rarely occurs.

I am excited by what we have learned so far but I am also humbled by how much we still need to know. Though one part of the research journey has ended, the new paths we have uncovered will provide an endless source of intellectual stimulation for us and others in the future. It has been a joy to have had the opportunity to travel the road of a research scientist examining the most complex process of all . . . behavior. I am certain that the next 25 years will be as intellectually stimulating and rewarding as the first 25!

Chronological List of Publications

Svare, B., and R. Gandelman (1973). Postpartum aggression in mice: Experiential and environmental factors. *Hormones and Behavior,* 4: 323–334.

Gandelman, R., and B. Svare (1974). Mice: Pregnancy termination, lactation, and aggression. *Hormones and Behavior,* 5: 397–405. *a*

Gandelman, R., and B. Svare (1974). Lactation following hysterectomy of pregnant mice. *Biology of Reproduction,* 12: 360–367. *b*

Svare, B., and R. Gandelman (1975). Postpartum aggression in mice: Inhibitory effect of estrogen. *Physiology and Behavior,* 14: 31–36.

Svare, B., and R. Gandelman (1976). Suckling stimulation induces aggression in virgin female mice. *Nature,* 320: 606–608. *a*

Svare, B., and R. Gandelman (1976). Postpartum aggression in mice: The influence of suckling stimulation. *Hormones and Behavior,* 7: 407–416. *b*

Svare, B., and R. Gandelman (1976). A longitudinal analysis of maternal aggression in Rockland-Swiss albino mice. *Developmental Psychobiology,* 9: 437–446. *c*

Svare, B. (1977). Maternal aggression in mice: Influence of the young. *Biobehavioral Reviews,* 1: 151–164.

Svare, B. (1979). Maternal aggression in mice: the nonspecific nature of the exteroceptive maintenance by young. *Aggressive Behavior,* 5: 417–424.

Svare, B. (1980). Testosterone propionate inhibits maternal aggression in mice. *Physiology and Behavior,* 24: 435–440.

Svare, B., M. Mann, and O. Samuels (1980). Mice: Suckling stimulation but not lactation important for maternal aggression. *Behavioral and Neural Biology*, 29: 453–462.

Mann, M., S. Michael, and B. Svare (1980). Ergot drugs suppress plasma prolactin and lactation but not aggressive behavior in parturient mice. *Hormones and Behavior*, 14: 319–329.

Svare, B., C. Beteridge, D. Katz, and O. Samuels (1981). Some situational and experiential determinants of maternal aggression in mice. *Physiology and Behavior*, 26: 253–258.

Broida, J., S. Michael, and B. Svare (1981). Plasma prolactin is not related to the initiation, maintenance, and decline of maternal aggression in mice. *Behavioral and Neural Biology*, 32: 121–125.

Svare, B. (1981). Maternal aggression in mammals. In: D.J. Gubernick and P. Klopfer (Eds.) *Parental Care in Mammals. New York*, Plenum Press, 179–210. *a*

Svare, B. (1981). Models of aggression employing female rodents. In P. Brain and D. Benton (Eds.). *The Biology of Aggression*.Netherlands: Nordhoff/Sigthoff, 503–508. *b*

Broida, J., and B. Svare (1982). Postpartum aggression in C57BL/6J and DBA/2J mice: Experiential and environmental influences. *Behavioral and Neural Biology*, 35: 76–83. *a*

Broida, J., and B. Svare (1982). Strain-typical patterns of pregnancy-induced nestbuilding in mice: Maternal and experiential influences. *Physiology and Behavior*, 29: 153–157. *b*

Mann, M., S.D. Michael, and B. Svare (1982). Ergot drugs suppress plasma levels of prolactin (PRL) but not growth hormone (GH), luteinizing hormone (LH) or corticosterone (CORT) in parturient mice. *Pharmacology, Biochemistry and Behavior*, 17: 837–840.

Svare, B., M. Mann, J. Broida, and S.D. Michael (1982). Maternal aggression exhibited by hypophysectomized parturient mice. *Hormones and Behavior*, 16: 455–461.

Mann, M., and B. Svare (1982). Factors influencing pregnancy-induced aggression in mice. *Behavioral and Neural Biology*, 36: 242–258.

Svare, B. (1983). Psychobiological determinants of maternal aggression in mice. In M. Hahn, E. Simmel, and C. Walters (Eds), *Genetic and Neural Aspects of Aggression: Synthesis and New Directions.* Lawrence Earlbaum, Hillsdale, New Jersey, 129–146.

Svare, B., and M. Mann (1983). Hormonal influences on maternal aggression in mammals. In B. Svare (Ed.) *Hormones and Aggressive Behavior. New York*, Plenum Press, 91–104. *a*

Mann, M.A., and B. Svare (1983) Prenatal testosterone exposure elevates maternal aggression in mice. *Physiology and Behavior*, 30: 503–507 *b*

Svare, B. (1983). *Hormones and Aggressive Behavior.* New York, Plenum Press.

Mann, M.A., J.L. Miele, C.H. Kinsley, and B. Svare (1983). Postpartum behavior in the mouse: The contribution of suckling stimulation to water intake, food intake, and body weight regulation. *Physiology and Behavior*, 31: 633–638.

Broida, J., and B. Svare (1983). Mice: Progesterone and the regulation of strain differences in pregnancy-induced nestbuilding. *Behavioral Neuroscience*, 97: 994–1004.

Mann, M.A., C. Konen, and B. Svare (1984). The role of progesterone in pregnancy-induced aggression in mice. *Hormones and Behavior*, 18: 140–160.

Broida, J., S.D. Michael, and B. Svare (1984). Acute endocrine correlates of attack by lactating females in male mice: Effects on plasma prolactin, luteinizing hormone and corticosterone levels. *Physiology and Behavior*, 32: 891–894.

Kinsley, C., J. Miele, L. Ghiraldi, C. Konen, and B. Svare (1986). Intrauterine position modulates maternal behaviors in female mice. *Physiology and Behavior*, 36: 793–799.

Svare, B., J. Miele, and C. Kinsley (1986). Mice: Progesterone stimulation of aggression in pregnancy-terminated females. *Hormones and Behavior*, 20: 194–200.

Konen, C., C. Kinsley, and B. Svare (1986). Mice: Postpartum aggression is elevated following prenatal progesterone exposure. *Hormones and Behavior*, 20:212–221.

Kinsley, C., and B. Svare (1987). Genotype modulates prenatal stress effects on aggression in male and female mice. *Behavioral and Neural Biology,* 47: 138–150.

Kinsley, C., and B. Svare (1988). Prenatal stress alters maternal aggression in female mice. *Physiology and Behavior,* 42: 7–13.

Svare, B. (1988). Genotype modulates the aggression promoting quality of progesterone in pregnant mice. *Hormones and Behavior,* 22: 90–99.

Garland, M., and B. Svare (1988). Suckling stimulation modulates the maintenance of postpartum aggression in mice. *Physiology and Behavior,* 44: 301–305.

Svare, B. (1989). Recent advances in the study of female aggressive behavior. In P.F. Brain, D. Mainardi, and S. Parmigiani (Eds), *House Mouse Aggression: A Model for Understanding the Evolution of Social Behavior.* Harwood Academic Publishers, Switzerland, 135–159.

Svare, B. (1990). Maternal aggression: Hormonal, genetic, and developmental determinants. In N. Krasnegor and R. Bridges (Eds), *Mammalian Parenting: Biochemical, Neurobiological, and Behavioral Determinants.* Oxford Press, New York, 135–154.

Ghiraldi, L., M. Plonsky and B. Svare (1993). Estrogen modulation of aggression in the peripartum period. *Hormones and Behavior,* 27: 251–268.

Svare, B., and M. Boechler (1994). Protection and abuse of young in mice: Influence of mother-young interactions. In S. Parmigiani and F. vom Saal, *Protection and Abuse of Young in Animals and Man.* Harwood: London, 465–476.

Svare, B., and M. Boechler (in press). Postpartum aggression in multiparous mice: Modulation by suckling and non-suckling stimuli. *Physiology and Behavior.*

Svare, B., and C. Kinsley (in preparation). Singleton female mice fail to show maternal aggression.

Index

Anogenital spacing
    defined, 85
    prenatal progesterone and, 96–97
    prenatal stress and, 91–94, 98
    prenatal testosterone and, 94–95

Bartke, Andrzej, 7–8
Basic research, 3
Beach, Frank, 11, 119
Behavioral endocrinology, 6–7
Boechler, Michael, 9
Broida, John, 9

Chance observations, 12
Continuous breeding colony, 12
Cross-fostering
    aggression and, 79

Drug screens
    aggression and, 120

Ergot drugs
    aggression and, 64–66
Estrogen
    nipple growth and, 60
    profiles during lactation, 26
    profiles during postpartum
        estrous, 26–27
    profiles during pregnancy, 26
    stimulation of aggression, 47
    suppression of aggression, 49–53
Exteroceptive stimuli
    and aggression, 31

Federal research grants
    applications for, 18
    bridge funding, 19–20
    compared to defense budget, 21
    Guggeheim Foundation, 17
    NIA, 17
    NIDA, 17
    NIH, 17
    NIMH, 17
    NSF, 17
    priority scores, 19
    renewals, 19
    resubmissions, 19
    review process for 18–19
    revision of 20
    study sections, 18–19
    success rates, 20
Feeding behavior
    ovarian hormones and, 27
Female aggression
    See maternal aggression,
        pregnancy-induced aggression,
        postpartum aggression
Fetal hormones
    aggression and, 85–86

Gandelman, Ron, 7
Genetic influences on aggression
    pospartum aggression, 78–83
    pregnancy-induced aggression,
        78–83
Ghiraldi, Loraina, 9
Graduate training, 6–7

Hypothalamus
    aggression and, 60–70
Hypophysectomy
    aggression and, 67–68
Hysterectomy
    aggression and, 41

Inbred mice
    aggression and, 77–83
Individual variation and
        aggression
    fetal hormones and, 85–86
    genes and, 78–83
    prior intrauterine position and,
        73–83
Intermale aggression, 14–15
Intrauterine position
    aggression and, 73–83
    estrous cycles and, 86
    fetal hormones and, 85–86
    learning and, 86
    terminology and, 85–87

Kinsley, Craig, 9

Laboratory-based research
    defined, 3
    in psychology 3–4
Lactation, 13, 27
Leshner, Alan, 6

Mann, Martha, 9
Maternal aggression
    See pregnancy-induced aggression
        and postpartum aggression
Maternal behavior
    and ovarian hormones, 27
Maternal defense
    See pregnancy-induced aggression
        and postpartum aggression
Methysergide
    postpartum aggression and, 69–70
Michael, Sandy, 64
Miele, Joe, 9
Misanin, Jim, 6

Nagy, Michael, 6
Neuroendocrine reflex arc
    and suckling, 61–63
    and aggression, 55–70
Nipples
    and aggression, 55–61
    removal of and aggression, 58
    growth of during pregnancy, 59
Nursing
    relationship to aggression, 56–58

Olfactory stimuli
    and aggression, 103–107
Optimization
    and aggression, 116–118
Ovarian hormones
    See also estrogen and proges-
        terone
    plasma profiles during preg-
        nancy, 26
    and nipple growth, 60
Parturition
    aggression and , 27
PCPA
    aggression and, 68–70

Postdoctoral training, 7–8
Postpartum aggression
    cross-fostering and 79
    drug screens and, 120
    ergot drugs and, 64–66
    exteroceptive control by young, 31
    genetic influences and, 78–83
    hypophysectomy and, 67–68
    individual variation and, 73–83
    methysergide and, 68–70
    neurotransmitters and, 68–70
    olfactory stimuli and, 103–107
    optimization and, 116–118
    PCPA and, 68–70
    prenatal stress and, 91–93
    prenatal progesterone and,
        96–97
    prenatal testosterone and, 94–95
    prolactin and, 61–68, 74
    prior intrauterine position and,
        85–90
    pup replacement and, 32
    relationship to male aggression,
        120
    relationship to postpartum blues,
        120
    reproductive experience and, 79
    role of young, 29–33
    serotonin and 68–70
    singleton fetuses and, 87–90
    topography of, 13–14, 25–28
Postpartum blues
    relationship to postpartum
        aggression, 120
Postpartum estrous
    and absence of aggression, 49–53
    defined, 27
Pregnancy
    detection of, 12
    hormonal changes during, 25–26
    termination and aggression,
        41–44

Pregnancy-induced aggression
    estrogen and, 47–48
    genetic influences and, 78–83
    hysterectomy and, 41
    individual variation and, 73–83
    olfactory stimuli and 103–107
    parturition and, 27
    pregnancy termination and, 41
    prenatal stress and, 91–93
    prior intrauterine position and,
        85–90
    progesterone levels and, 74–75
    progesterone replacement and,
        42–46, 82
    topography of, 25–27
Prenatal progesterone
    aggression and, 96–97
    anogenital distance and, 96–97
Prenatal stress
    aggression and, 91–93
    effects on anogenital distance,
        91–94
Prenatal testosterone
    aggression and, 94–95
    anogenital distance and, 94–95
Progesterone
    implants and aggression, 41–46,
        81–83
    nipple growth and, 60
    pregnancy-induced aggression
        and, 41
    prenatal exposure to, 96–97
    profiles during lactation, 26–27
    profiles during pregnancy,
        26–28
Prolactin
    aggression and, 61–68
    ergot drugs and, 61–63
    secretion during lactation, 28
    secretion during pregnancy, 28
Proximate causation
    defined, 35–37

Proximate causation (*continued*)
  olfactory stimuli and, 103–107
  summary of, 109–112
Pup replacment
  and aggression, 32

Radioimmunoassay of hormones,
  26
Reproductive experience
  maternal aggression and, 79
Rockland-Swiss mice, 12

Serotonin
  and aggression, 68–70
Sexual behavior
  ovarian hormones and, 27
Singleton fetuses
  aggression and, 87
SUNY-Albany, 8–9
Svare, Bruce,
  Bucknell University, 6
  Gardner High School, 5
  Rutgers University, 6
  SUNY-Albany, 8–9
  Susquehanna University, 5–6
  Worcester Foundation, 7

Thelectomy
  postpartum aggression and,
    55–61
Topography of aggression
  postpartum aggression, 13–14,
    25–28
  pregnancy-induced aggression,
    25–27

Ultimate causation
  defined, 36–37
  summary of and aggression,
    113–118

Vaginal plug, 12
Virgin females
  hormonal induction of aggression
    and, 59–61, 82

Weaning, 13

Young
  role of in postpartum aggression,
    29–33